James H. Humphrey, EdD

Child Development Through Sports

Pre-publication
REVIEW

"This book is designed for all parents, youth sports coaches, and elementary school teachers responsible for providing physical education classes. James Humphrey has clearly brought theory into practice in a logical as well as focused manner related to the role that sports can play in the total development of the unified child. This book addresses four topics that make it a must-read for parents, youth sports coaches, and those who provide physical education programming to elementary-aged children: development of the (1) physical, (2) social, (3) emotional, and (4) intellectual needs of children and guidelines on how to meet those needs through sports."

Ron French, EdD, CAPE
Professor, Department of Kinesiology,
Texas Woman's University,
Denton

Child Development
Through Sports

THE HAWORTH PRESS
Titles of Related Interest

Integrating Exercise, Sports, Movement, and Mind: Therapeutic Unity edited by Kate F. Hays

Strategic Planning for Collegiate Athletics by Deborah A. Yow, R. Henry Migliore, William W. Bowden, Robert E. Stevens, and David L. Loudon

Stress in College Athletics: Causes, Consequences, Coping by James H. Humphrey, Deborah A. Yow, and William W. Bowden

Parents, Children, and Adolescents: Interactive Relationships and Development in Context by Anne-Marie Ambert

Child Development Through Sports

James H. Humphrey, EdD

The Haworth Press®
New York • London • Oxford

The Haworth Press, Inc., 10 Alice Street, Binghamton, NY 13904-1580.

Cover design by Marylouise E. Doyle.

Library of Congress Cataloging-in-Publication Data

Humphrey, James Harry, 1911-
   Child development through sports / James H. Humphrey.
      p. cm.
Includes bibliographical references and index.
   ISBN 0-7890-1827-6 (hardcover : alk. paper)—ISBN 0-7890-1828-4 (softcover : alk. paper)
1. Sports for children. 2. Child development. I. Title.
   GV709.2 .H845 2003
   796' .083—dc21
                                          2002012590

CONTENTS

Foreword

It is a pleasure to contribute a foreword to Professor James H. Humphrey's latest contribution to our understanding of children and their physical activity. In this book, Dr. Humphrey has focused his attention on children and sports. This is an important issue in our society today. Parents listen to the stories of Tiger Woods learning to play golf before he could ride a bicycle, or they watch Olympians tell how they have practiced and competed throughout most of their youth in order to win a gold medal. The message seems clear—start early and practice long hours with an excellent coach. Clearly, the stories of elite athletes who achieve incredible success are the extreme examples. But with organized youth sports starting at age five or sometimes younger, parents and caregivers are faced with difficult decisions. At what age should children begin playing organized sports? What sports are best? How many sports? How often? What is a good program? These are not easy questions, and in this book Dr. Humphrey offers a careful analysis of these problems and a thoughtful guide for answering such questions.

Children love to play, to be physical. Their exuberance when confronted with a new playground or a sandy beach is obvious. Contrast this carefree image of children at play with the scenes of those same children playing in an organized sporting event. The playful spirit has been replaced by the seriousness of a competitive game. Children are in the spotlight, their skills scrutinized by those watching. Children cheer when they win, but they are easily overwhelmed by their own or the team's failure. Dr. Humphrey, who has been writing on child development for years, offers his thoughts on how best to maximize a child's development. Sports can provide a unique and important context for children to develop their social, emotional, physical, and intellectual capabilities.

Children playing sports is an integral part of our culture. The question is not really whether children should participate but how best to help them develop through their sporting experiences. Dr. Humphrey presents his thoughts on navigating the risks and benefits so that sporting experiences can serve the best interests of children. This is a valuable book and one that parents, coaches, and those adults responsible for children and sports should read.

Jane E. Clark, PhD
Professor and Chairperson
Department of Kinesiology
University of Maryland, College Park

Preface

For the better part of six decades I have been involved in children's sports as a participant, observer, parent, teacher, and coach. Over the years, I have had an opportunity to experience firsthand the potential contribution that sports participation can make to child development. The key word here is *potential* because any benefit that children receive from participation in sports does not accrue automatically. Indeed, there is an ugly side to sports participation that can have a negative impact on the lives of children if programs are not conducted in an appropriate manner.

Therefore, it is the purpose of this book to explore the many aspects of children's sports. Along with my own personal experience in this area, I have consulted with both proponents and critics of children's sports, which included parents, professional athletes, coaches, school personnel, and children themselves. I have tried to merge all of this information into what I hope will be a sensible and compelling guide for those adults—parents, coaches, and other significant adults—who are involved, or plan to become involved, in children's sports in a way that will be in the best interest of the child.

Chapter 1 is an overview of child development, with emphasis on the total developmental concept. Chapters 2 and 3 give consideration to the areas of health and stress as important factors in child development. Chapter 4 presents an overview of children's sports including emphasis on such aspects as competition, injuries, supervision, interests, and benefits. In Chapter 5, developmental objectives of children's sports are taken into account. Chapters 6 through 9 go into some detail with reference to physical, social, emotional, and intellectual development of children through sports.

A book is seldom the sole product of the author. It is almost always true that many individuals participate, at least indirectly, in some way before a book is completed. Such is the case here. In this regard, I would like to thank the hundreds of children and adults who provided essential information by responding to my extensive surveys and interviews.

Finally, I owe a personal debt of gratitude to Dr. Jane E. Clark, who made a painstaking effort to evaluate and critically appraise the manuscript from the point of view of a child development specialist.

ABOUT THE AUTHOR

James H. Humphrey, EdD, is Professor Emeritus of the Department of Kinesiology at the University of Maryland. He was a charter member and the first chairman-elect of the Research Council of the American School Health Association. Dr. Humphrey received the National Honor Award from the American Alliance for Health, Physical Education, Recreation, and Dance in 1972. The following year, he was elected to membership in the Society of Children's Book Writers and was selected for the International Compendium of Eminent People in the Field of Exceptional Education.

Dr. Humphrey has authored or co-authored more than 50 books, including *Stress in College Athletics: Causes, Consequences, Coping* (Haworth Press). His writings and research reports have appeared in more than 20 national and international journals and magazines, and he is listed in the *International Authors and Writers Who's Who* and *Contemporary Authors of Meritorious Works.*

Chapter 1

An Overview of Child Development

Child development is defined as, "an interdisciplinary approach to the study of children, drawing upon such sciences as biology, physiology, embryology, pediatrics, sociology, psychiatry, anthropology, and psychology. Emphasis is placed on the importance of understanding: children through study of their mental, emotional, social, and physical, growth. Particular emphasis is laid on the appraisal of the impacts on the growing personality of home, school, and community."[1] Although this definition applies to children of all ages, this book focuses on elementary school—those approximately five to twelve years old, in kindergarten through grade six.

Many child educational leaders agree that the goal of elementary education is to stimulate and guide the *development* of children so that they will function in life activities involving vocation, citizenship, and enriched leisure; and, further, so that they will possess as high a level of physical, social, emotional, and intellectual well-being as their individual capacities will permit. More succinctly stated, the purpose of such education should be in the direction of *total development* of children throughout the formative years.

Teachers, parents, and other adults who deal in some way with children must explore the developmental processes as they relate to the education of children.

GENERAL CHARACTERISTICS OF FIVE- TO TWELVE-YEAR-OLD CHILDREN

As five- to twelve-year-old children progress through the various stages of development, certain distinguishing characteristics can be identified that suggest implications for the developmental process.

(The characteristics given here are general in nature and will be discussed in detail in subsequent chapters.)

Ages Five to Eight

From age five to eight, children begin their formal education. Not only are these children taking an important step toward becoming increasingly more independent and self-reliant, but as they learn they also move from being highly self-centered individuals to becoming more socialized members of the group.

The urge to action is expressed through movement since the child lives in a "movement world." Children at these age levels thrive on vigorous activity, developing as they climb, run, jump, hop, skip, or keep time to music. An important physical aspect at this age level is that the eyeball is increasing in size and the eye muscles are still developing. This factor is an important determinant in the child's readiness to see and read small print, and, thus, it involves a sequence from large print on charts to primer type in preprimers and primers.

Even though five- to eight-year-old children have a relatively short attention span, they are extremely curious about their environment. Adults can capitalize upon this urge to learn by providing opportunities to gain information from firsthand experiences through the use of the senses. The child sees, hears, smells, feels, tastes, and moves in order to learn.

Ages Nine to Ten

From age nine to ten is the period that usually marks the time spent in third and fourth grades. These children have a wider range of interests and a longer attention span. Although strongly individualistic, they work more as a group. Organized games afford opportunities for developing and practicing skills in good leadership and followership as well as in body control, strength, and endurance. Small muscles are developing, manipulative skills are increasing, and muscular coordination is improving. The eyes have developed to a point where many children can and do read more widely. Children are more capable of getting information from books and are beginning to learn more through vicarious experiences. This is the stage in development when skills of communication (listening, speaking, reading, and writing) and the number system are needed to deal with situations both in and out of school.

Ages Ten to Twelve

From ten to twelve most children complete the fifth and sixth grades. This is a period of transition as they go from childhood into the preadolescent periods of their development. They may show concern over bodily changes and are sometimes self-conscious about appearance. These children tend to differ widely in physical maturation and emotional stability. Rate of physical growth can be rapid, sometimes showing itself in poor posture and restlessness. It is essential to recognize that prestige among peers is likely to be more important than adult approval. During this period, children are ready for a higher level of intellectual skills that involve reasoning, discerning fact from opinion, noting cause-and-effect relationships, drawing conclusions, and using various references to locate and compare validity of information. They are beginning to show more proficiency in expressing oral and written communication.

FORMS OF DEVELOPMENT

During the years of kindergarten through sixth grade, children develop (1) *socially,* from self-centered individuals to participating members of the group; (2) *emotionally,* from a state manifesting anger outbursts to a higher degree of self-control; (3) *physically,* from childhood to the brink of adolescence; and (4) *intellectually,* from learning by firsthand experience to learning from technical and specialized resources. If children are educated as growing organisms, aspects of development need the utmost consideration in planning and guiding learning experiences that will be most beneficial for them at a particular stage of development.

Other forms of development can be subclassified under one of these areas. For example, *motor development* (a progressive change in motor performance) can be considered part of the broader aspect of physical development. In addition, *moral development* (the capacity of the individual to distinguish between standards of right and wrong) could be considered a dimension of the broader aspect of social development. This is to say that moral development involving achievement in ability to determine right from wrong is influential in the individual's social behavior.

Other terminology is sometimes used to describe forms of development. Reference is made to the *learning domains,* which consist of the *affective* domain, the *cognitive* domain, and the *psychomotor* domain. *Affective development* is ordinarily thought of as being concerned with "appreciation," and it is sometimes referred to as socioemotional development, a combination of two of the four main forms. *Cognitive development* in this context means knowledge or understanding. *Psychomotor development* involves learning to move with control and efficiency or, more simply stated, skill in movement.

A CONCEPT OF TOTAL CHILD DEVELOPMENT

Experimental evidence indicates that a human being must be considered as a whole and not a collection of parts. This means that a child is a unified individual, or what is more commonly known as the *whole* child.

Total development encompasses the various major forms of development. All of these components—physical, social, emotional, and intellectual—are highly interrelated and interdependent. All are of importance to well-being. The condition of any one of these forms of development affects all other forms to a degree and, thus, development as a whole. When a nervous child stutters or becomes nauseated, a mental state is not necessarily causing a physical symptom. On the contrary, a pressure imposed upon the child causes a series of reactions, which includes thought, verbalization, digestive processes, and muscular function. It is not always true that the mind causes the body to become upset; the total organism is upset by a particular situation and reflects its upset in several ways, including disturbances in thought, feeling, and bodily processes. The whole child responds to the social and physical environment, and as he or she is affected by the environment, the child in turn has an effect upon it.

However, since physical *or* intellectual development, rather than physical *and* intellectual development, has been glorified, we divide the two in our minds. The result of this kind of thinking may be that we sometimes pull human beings apart. Separating the mind and body can lead to unbalanced development of the child with respect to mind and body and/or social adjustment.

The previous statements point out that the identified components of total development constitute the unified individual. The fact that each of these aspects might well be considered as a separate entity should also be taken into account. As such, each warrants a separate discussion, in order to fully understand the place of each as an integral part of total development.

Physical Development

One point of departure in discussing physical development could be to state that "everybody has a body." Some are short, some are tall, some are lean, and some are fat. Children come in different sizes, but all of them are born with certain capacities that are influenced by the environment.

It might be said of children that they "are" their bodies. It is something they can see. It is their base of operation. The other components of total development—social, emotional, and intellectual—are somewhat vague where children are concerned. Although these are manifested in various ways, children do not always see them as they do the physical aspect. Consequently, it becomes important that children be helped early in life to gain control over the physical aspect, or what is known as *basic body control*. The ability to do this, of course, will vary from one child to another. It will likely depend upon the status of *physical fitness* of each child.

Physical fitness is a broad area and can be broken down into certain components: muscular strength, endurance, and power; circulatory-respiratory endurance; speed; flexibility; balance; and coordination. These components can be measured by calibrated instruments, such as measurements of muscular strength. Moreover, we can tell how tall children are or how heavy they are at any stage of their development. Other accurate data can be derived with assessments of blood pressure, blood counts, urinalysis, etc.

Social Development

Human beings are social beings. They work together for the benefit of society and have fought together in times of national emergency to preserve the kind of society they believe in. Although all this may be true, social development is still quite vague and confusing, particularly where children are concerned.

It was easy to identify the components of physical fitness since they are the same for children as for adults. However, this does not necessarily hold true for the social aspect. The components of social fitness for children may be different from those for adults. Some adults consider children social misfits because their behavior might not be socially acceptable to other adults.

Young children are uninhibited in their social development, and we need to be concerned with their social maturity. We need to consider certain characteristics of social maturity and how well they are dealt with at the different stages of child development. Are we helping children become self-reliant by giving them independence at the proper time? Are we helping them to be outgoing and interested in others as well as themselves? Are we helping them to know how to satisfy their own needs in a socially desirable way? Are we helping them to develop a wholesome attitude toward themselves and others?

Emotional Development

For many years, emotional development has been a difficult concept to define. In addition, there have been many changing ideas and theories in the study of emotion. There are pleasant and unpleasant emotions. For example, joy could be considered a pleasant emotional experience, and fear would be an unpleasant one. It is interesting to note that a great deal of the literature is devoted to emotions that are unpleasant. For example, in books on psychology more space is given to fear, hate, and guilt than to love, sympathy, and contentment.

Generally speaking, the pleasantness or unpleasantness of an emotion seems to be determined by its strength or intensity, by the nature of the situation arousing it, and by the way a child perceives or interprets the situation. The emotions of young children tend to be more intense than those of adults. If adults are not aware of this aspect of child behavior, they will not understand why a child reacts rather strongly to a situation that to them seems somewhat insignificant. The fact that children will react differently to the same type of situation should also be taken into account. For example, something that might anger one child might have a rather passive influence on another.

Intellectual Development

The word *intelligence* is derived from the Latin word *intellectus,* which literally means the "power of knowing." Intelligence can be defined in many ways. One general description of it is *the capacity to learn or understand.*

Children possess various degrees of intelligence, and most fall within a range of what is called "normal" intelligence. In dealing with this we should perhaps give attention to what might be called *intellectual fitness.* However, this is difficult to do. Because of the somewhat vague nature of intelligence, it is practically impossible to identify specific components of it. Thus, we need to view intellectual fitness in a somewhat different manner.

For purposes of this discussion, I will consider intellectual fitness from two different but closely related points of view—first, from a standpoint of intellectual needs and second, from a standpoint of how certain things influence intelligence. If a child's intellectual needs are being met, perhaps we could also say that he or she is intellectually fit. From the second point of view, if we know how certain things influence intelligence then we might understand better how to contribute to intellectual fitness by improving upon some of these factors.

There is general agreement among child development specialists with regard to the intellectual needs of children, which include (1) a need for challenging experiences at the child's level of ability, (2) a need for intellectually successful and satisfying experiences, and (3) a need for the opportunity to participate in creative experiences instead of always having to conform. Some of the factors that tend to influence intelligence are (1) health and physical condition, (2) emotional disturbance, and (3) certain social and economic factors. When teachers, parents, and other adults understand the intellectual needs and factors that influence intelligence, they are able to help children with their intellectual pursuits.

MEETING THE NEEDS OF CHILDREN

In discussing needs of children it is important to consider their *interests* as well. Although needs and interests are closely related and highly interdependent, certain important differences need to be taken into account.

Needs of children, particularly those of an individual nature, are likely to be innate. Interests may be acquired as products of the environment. A child may demonstrate an interest in a certain unsafe practice that is obviously not in accord with his or her needs at a certain age level. The two-year-old may be interested in climbing the stairs, but this may result in injury. Acquiring a particular interest because of environmental conditions is further illustrated in the case of children coming from families that are superstitious about certain kinds of foods or certain foods eaten in combination. In such cases, acquiring an interest from other family members might build up a lifetime resistance to a certain kind of food that is very nutritious and beneficial to the child's physical needs.

Obtaining a proper balance between needs and interests is very important. However, arriving at a suitable ratio between them is not an easy task. Although we should undoubtedly think first in terms of meeting a child's needs, we must also consider his or her interests. A general principle by which we might be guided is that the *lower* the age level of children, the more we should take the responsibility for meeting their needs. This is based on the obvious assumption that the younger the child, the less experience he or she has had, and consequently there is less opportunity to develop certain interests.

Classification of Needs

Children's needs have been classified in many ways, and it should be kept in mind that a classification of needs is usually made arbitrarily for a specific purpose. For example, when speaking of biological and psychological needs it should be understood that each of these, although classified separately, is interdependent. I use the same terms for classification of needs as for the forms of development, that is, physical, social, emotional, and intellectual needs. (In subsequent chapters I discuss these needs in greater detail.)

HELPING CHILDREN UNDERSTAND
THEIR OWN DEVELOPMENT

In recent years there has been an increasing sentiment among young men and women of high school and college age that they have a need to *find* themselves. This should fortify the notion that one of the most important aspects of the "growing up" years is that children develop an understanding of themselves. This can be accomplished to some extent when adults improve upon their knowledge about children and, perhaps more important, prepare to use this knowledge with children as they grow and develop.

As much as possible, parents and teachers should provide an environment in the home and school that is a stable sanctuary which the child knows will be there when needed. Children need to be accepted for themselves, with their own unique abilities and limitations. They need to be permitted to grow and learn at their own rate and in their own way—and not to be made to feel inadequate in developing and learning even though they may not conform themselves to some standard or norm. They need to identify themselves as distinct individuals, and their uniqueness is deserving of respect. As children mature, they should have the opportunity to assume independence and responsibilities that are commensurate with their age and abilities.

Children require control and discipline that is consistent, reasonable, and understandable to them. A few clear and simple rules are usually entirely adequate and tend to give children a feeling of security in that they know what they can and cannot do. Therefore, it may be said that children need defined limits to prevent them from destructive behavior and perhaps from even destroying themselves. It is important to emphasize that consistency in all aspects of the environment is very important. For example, acts for which they are ignored, praised, or punished should not vary from time to time. If this feedback varies, children are likely to become confused and their adjustment will be made more difficult. Similarly, expressions of love should not be spasmodic, nor should the threat of withdrawal of love ever be used as a weapon to control behavior.

A standard dictionary lists almost 400 hyphenated words beginning with *self*—from self-abandonment to self-worth. The discussion here will be concerned with self-image, or how a person conceives himself or herself or his or her role. Reflecting back to the comments on physical development, recall the suggestion that where children are concerned, *they are their bodies;* that is, children are essentially concerned with the *physical self.* It is something they can see and is much more meaningful to them than the social, emotional, or intellectual *self.* This being the case, attention is now turned to what will be called *body image,* which is the child's picture of his or her bodily person and his or her abilities. It has been clearly demonstrated that when adults help children improve upon body image, a basic understanding of the broader aspect of self will more likely be established.

Determining Deficiencies in Body Image

One of the first steps is to determine if a child has problems with body image. There is no foolproof method of detecting this because many mannerisms said to be indicative of body image problems can also be the same for other deficiencies. Nevertheless, adults should be on the alert to certain possible deficiencies.

There are two ways in which deficiencies concerned with body image can be detected: (1) by observing certain behaviors and (2) by employing some relatively simple diagnostic techniques. The following list contains examples of both possibilities.

1. Ask children to make a drawing of themselves. The primary reason for this is to see if certain parts of the body are not included in the drawing.

2. A child with a lack of body image may manifest tenseness in movements or be unsure of the movements. For example, if the child is instructed to move a body part such as placing one foot forward, he or she may direct attention to the body part before making the movement. Or he or she may look at another child to observe the movement before attempting to make the movement. This could also possibly be due to poor processing of the input (auditory or visual stimulus) provided for the movement.

3. When instructed to use one body part the child may also move the corresponding body part when it is not necessary. For example, when asked to swing the right arm he or she may also start swinging the left arm simultaneously.

4. In such activities as catching an object, the child may turn toward the object when this is not necessary. For example, when a thrown beanbag approaches the child, he or she may move forward with either side of the body rather than trying to retrieve the beanbag with the hands as both feet remain stationary.

Improving upon Body Image

The following activities can be used with children for diagnosis of lack of body image, body-image improvement, evaluation of body-image status, or various combinations of these factors. Some of the activities are age-old, and others have been developed for specific conditions.

Busy Bee

Over the years I have conducted experiments in an attempt to determine the effect of participation in certain body-movement activities on body image. The following is an example of this approach, utilizing the game Busy Bee. This experiment was conducted with five- and six-year-old children.

In this game, the children are placed in pairs facing each other and dispersed around the activity area. One child, the caller, is in the center of the area. This child makes calls such as "shoulder to shoulder," "toe to toe," or "hand to hand." (In the early stages of the game, it might be a good idea for the adult to do the calling.) As the calls are made, the paired children go through the appropriate motions with their partners. After a few calls, the caller will shout, "Busy Bee!" This is the signal for every child to get a new partner, including the caller. The child who does not get a partner can name the new caller.

As the children play the game, make them aware of the location of various parts of the body in order to develop the concept of full-body image. Before the game is played, ask the children to draw a picture of themselves. Many may not know how to begin, and others may omit some of the major limbs in their drawings. After playing Busy Bee, ask the children to again draw a picture of themselves. This time they should be more successful. All of the drawings should have bodies, heads, arms, and legs. Some of them may have hands, feet, eyes, and ears. A few may even have teeth and hair.

Come with Me

Several children form a circle, with one child outside of it. He or she walks around the circle, taps another child, and says, "Come with me." The child tapped falls in behind the first child and they continue walking around the circle. The second child taps a child and says, "Come with me." This continues until several children have been tapped. At a given point the first child calls out, "Go home!" On this signal all the children try to get back to their original place in the circle. The first child also tries to get into one of these places. There will be one child left out. He or she can be the first child for the next game.

In the early stages of this game the adult should call out where each child is to be tapped. For example, "on the arm," "on the leg," etc. After a time, the child doing the tapping can call out where he or she is going to tap. The adult can observe whether the children are tapped in the proper places.

Mirrors

One child is selected as the leader and stands facing a line of children. This child goes through a variety of movements and the children in the line try to do the same thing; that is, they act as mirrors. The leader should be changed frequently.

In this activity, the children become aware of different body parts and movements. The adult should observe how well and how quickly the children are able to copy the movements of the leader.

Change Circles

Several circles are drawn on the floor or outdoor activity area with one less circle than the number of participants. The one child who does not have a circle is "It" and stands in the middle of the area. The adult calls out signals in the form of body parts. For example, such calls could include "hands on knees," "hand on head," "right hand on left foot," etc. After a time, the adult calls out, "Change circles" whereupon all the children try to get into a different circle. The child who is "It" also tries to find a circle. The child who does not find a circle can be "It" or a new person can be chosen to be "It."

The adult should observe closely to see how the children react to the calls and whether they are looking at the other children for clues. As time goes on and the children become more familiar with their body parts, more complicated calls can be made.

Body Tag

In this game one child is selected to be "It." He or she chases the other children and attempts to tag one of them. If successful, the child tagged can become "It." If "It" does not succeed within a reasonable amount of time, a new "It" can be selected. In order to be officially tagged, a specific part of the body must be tagged by "It." Thus, the game could be shoulder tag, arm tag, or leg tag as desired.

The adult observes the child to see whether he or she tags the correct body part. To add more interest to the activity, the child can call out the part of the body to be tagged during each session of the game.

Summary

These are just a few of the possibilities for improving upon body image and, thus, an understanding of self. Creative adults should be able to think of numerous others that could satisfy this purpose. These activities have been field-tested with large numbers of children and have been found to be very successful in improving body image.

Chapter 2

Health As a Factor in Child Development

The health of a child is one of the most important factors in his or her development. Yet the comparatively low expenditures for life values such as education and health make it clear that our national priorities could be subject to question as far as the welfare of our children is concerned. This lack of concern for optimum health of children can seriously impact their development.

THE MEANING OF HEALTH AND RELATED TERMS

The meaning of *health* depends upon the particular frame of reference in which it is used. It has been a relatively common practice to think of health in terms of the condition of a normally functioning living organism. This idea is still accepted by many people. In subscribing to this particular concept, these individuals tend to think of health predominantly as a state in which there is absence of disease, pain, or symptoms related to a poorly functioning organism.

Health is now being considered more and more in terms of *well-being,* which is perhaps our most important human value. In this point of view, the ideal state of health would be one in which all of the various parts of the human organism function at an optimum level at all times. Although it is very unlikely that the human organism will ever achieve the ideal state suggested here, such a level is ordinarily used as a standard for diagnosing or appraising the human health status.

Considering health in terms of absence of disease places it in a negative sense. The well-being concept places positive emphasis on the term. It seems logical to assume that modern society's goal should be directed toward achieving the highest level of well-being for all of its citizens.

In view of the previous discussion, it is interesting to note the results of my own health surveys of nine- and ten-year-old children. When asked what the word *health* meant, 70 percent answered that it was concerned with the condition of the body (for example, "when your body is in good condition" and "to be in good shape"). Twenty percent identified health specifically with eating the right foods (for example, "when you eat the proper foods"). And 10 percent identified health specifically with exercise (for example, "when you get lots of exercise").

Health Knowledge, Attitudes, and Practice

Any discussion of the meaning of health should consider the three aspects of health: knowledge, attitudes, and practice. Each of these dimensions will be dealt with separately, but it is important at the outset to consider them together for the purpose of better understanding how they are related.

Health Knowledge

In order to benefit most from health-knowledge experiences, these experiences should develop into desirable health practices. The ultimate goal should be a kind of behavior that will ensure optimum present and future health for the individual. However, before the most desirable and worthwhile health practices can be achieved there is a need for a certain amount of desirable health knowledge and a proper attitude.

Although it is obvious that *to know* is not necessarily *to do,* that which is done wisely will depend upon the kind and amount of health knowledge a person has acquired. In accumulation of health knowledge, he or she will need to understand *why* it is beneficial to follow a certain practice. When the person knows why, it is perhaps more likely that a desirable *attitude* toward certain health practices will be developed. If he or she has a sufficient amount of desirable health knowledge developed through valid health concepts, and also a proper attitude, the individual will be more apt to apply the knowledge to health behavior. Moreover, he or she should be in a better position to exercise good judgment and make wise decisions in matters pertaining to health if the right kind and amount of health knowledge has been obtained.

The scope of health knowledge is endless, and it would be impossible to learn all there is to know about it. However, certain basic concepts about health should be developed by individuals at all age levels. Generally speaking, the individual should acquire knowledge pertaining to the direct basic needs of the human organism and, in addition, knowledge regarding the organism as it functions in its environment.

Knowledge about health is acquired in a variety of different ways. Some of it is the product of tradition and, as such, oftentimes is nothing more than folklore. Certain popular notions about health that have long since been dispelled by the scientific community are still held by many people who have not, for some reason or other, benefited from modern health knowledge.

Other kinds of health knowledge are derived through mass communication media such as television and radio. Although some of this information may be valid, individuals should be alert to the possibility that the primary purpose of many kinds of advertising is to sell a product that proclaims results which are not always likely to be attainable.

Another source of health knowledge is the home. In fact, most health knowledge starts in the home. Parents are our first teachers, and what we learn from them tends to remain with us. A home contributes much to the health knowledge of children simply by providing good meals and a friendly, well-regulated, but pleasant and recreationally challenging environment in which to grow. Children who do not benefit from good home experiences receive their first source of health knowledge in school.

At what age is a child capable of acquiring health knowledge? A 1988 study by Gary D. Nelson of the Centers for Disease Control and Prevention in Atlanta, Georgia, showed that when children were presented with health-knowledge learning experiences at the preschool level, their health knowledge increased.[1] This study examined the effects of the "Hale and Hardy's Helpful Health Hints" preschool health education curriculum on the health knowledge of children three to five years old, residing in Alabama. The data-producing sample in the study consisted of nine experimental preschool programs (194 children) and three comparison group programs (seventy-three children). A picture identification test was used to assess each child's pretest and posttest health knowledge of curriculum content including the five senses, safety, nutrition, dental health, personal responsibility, emotions, hygiene, and drugs/medicines. Posttest knowledge scores increased by 22 percent among experimental group preschool programs and 12 percent among comparison group preschool programs.

Health Attitudes

Any discussion of attitudes requires an identification of the meaning of the term. Although it is recognized that people will attach different meanings to the term *attitude,* I think of attitude as being associated with feelings. Expressions such as, "How do you feel about it?" imply, "What is your *attitude* toward it?" Therefore, attitude could be considered a factor in the determination of action because of this feeling about something. For example, knowledge alone that physical exercise is beneficial will not necessarily lead to regular exercising, but a strong feeling or attitude about it might be a determining factor that leads a person to exercise regularly.

There is little evidence to support unequivocally the contention that attitude has a positive direct influence on behavior. One of the difficulties in studying this phenomenon scientifically lies in the questionable validity of instruments used to measure attitudes. Moreover, there is little consistent agreement with regard to the meaning of attitudes. Thus, the position taken here is one of theoretical postulation based upon logical assumption.

Health attitudes could well be considered a gap that exists between health knowledge and health practice, and this gap needs to be bridged if effective health behavior is to result. For example, a person who has acquired some knowledge regarding the degree to which cigarette smoking can be harmful to his or her health will have some sort of underlying feeling toward such knowledge. He or she may choose to disregard it because friends have assumed such an attitude toward it, or he or she may feel that the evidence is convincing enough to believe that cigarette smoking is something he or she can avoid. In either case, an attitude has been developed toward the practice of cigarette smoking, and it is likely that a person may react in accordance with this feeling. It should also be mentioned that an individual may not necessarily react with true feeling because it may be considered fashionable to smoke cigarettes so as not to lose status with friends who do. (This is a strong possibility as far as some children are concerned.) However a person chooses to react will be tempered by the consequences associated with the knowledge acquired about cigarette smoking.

Obviously, it would be hoped that the accumulation of health knowledge would be accompanied by a positive attitude, which would result in taking desirable action. It is possible that only in terms of such a positive attitude are desirable health practices and a better way of living likely to result.

Health Practice

Many people do not capitalize on the knowledge they have acquired. They act only on impulse and their actions are influenced to an extent by their friends. However, in matters as important as health, it it is hoped that they weigh the facts and scientific evidence before acting, looking at health practices that are desirable and those that are undesirable, and those that will result in pleasantness or unpleasantness.

Altering behavior is not always an easy matter; however, it is hoped that individuals will want to make a positive modification of their own health behavior after acquiring desirable health knowledge and forming favorable attitudes. In the final analysis, the individual will make the decisions regarding his or her own health practices. In young children, perhaps these health practices can be forced, although this notion is impractical if we are to expect the best learning to take place. Forcing health practices on children as they grow older not only appears impractical but in many cases unwarranted as well. It is likely this same philosophy can be applied to adults.

As far as personal health is concerned, it becomes a matter of how much risk a person is willing to take, and health practices are likely to be based on this factor. By way of illustration, I refer again to cigarette smoking and health. To my knowledge, it has never been demonstrated scientifically that cigarette smoking is in any way beneficial to the physical health of the human organism. On the contrary, there has been a great deal of medical evidence which indicates that smoking can contribute to certain types of serious diseases. Yet, untold numbers of individuals are willing to assume a dangerous risk in defiance of such evidence. After a person has learned about some aspect of health, he or she is faced with a choice. It is hoped that the chosen course of health action would involve a minimum of risk.

In my studies of nine- to ten-year-old children, I asked them to identify what they considered were *good* and *bad* health practices. An overwhelming 86 percent said eating proper foods was a good health practice. Foods most frequently mentioned were milk and fruits and vegetables. Ten percent said taking the right medicine was a good health practice, 2 percent said wearing warm clothes, and 2 percent said exercising.

As far as bad health practices are concerned, 55 percent said eating improper foods, some of which were candy, sugar, fats, and the broad classification of "junk foods." (Interestingly enough, the latter is very popular, at least among ten- to eleven-year-olds.) The remaining 45 percent felt that the worst health practice was substance abuse and cited such things as taking drugs, smoking, and drinking.

THE HEALTH TRIANGLE

In discussing the subject of caring for health I like to deal with what I call the "health triangle": (1) nutrition and diet, (2) rest and sleep, and (3) physical activity and exercise.

Nutrition and Diet

Nutrition and diet are highly interrelated and interdependent. However, certain differences need to be taken into account, particularly as far as the meaning of these two areas is concerned.

Nutrition

Nutrition can be described as the sum of the processes by which a person takes in and utilizes food substances; that is, the nourishment of the body by food. These processes consist of ingestion, digestion, absorption, and assimilation.

Ingestion is derived from the Latin word *ingestus,* meaning to take in. In this context, it means taking in food, or the act of eating. The process of *digestion* involves breaking down and converting food into substances that can be *absorbed* through the lining of the intestinal tract and into the blood and used by the body. *Assimilation* is concerned with incorporating or converting nutrients into protoplasm, which is the essential material making up living cells.

The body needs many essential nutrients from foods to keep it functioning properly. These nutrients fall into the broad groups of proteins, carbohydrates, fats, vitamins, and minerals. Although water is not a nutrient in the strictest sense of the word, it must be included, for nutrition cannot take place without it.

Three major functions of nutrients are building and repairing all body tissues, regulating all body functions, and providing fuel for the body's energy needs. Although all nutrients can do their best work when they are combined with other nutrients, each still has its own vital role to play.

Digestion. The digestive system of the body is more than thirty feet long from beginning to end, and the chemical processes that occur within the walls of this mucus-lined hollow tube are extremely complex in nature. From the moment that food is taken into the mouth until waste products are excreted, the body's chemical laboratory is at work. The principal parts of this system are the elements of the alimentary canal, consisting of the oral cavity, pharynx, esophagus, stomach, small intestine, and large intestine. Two additional organs are necessary to complete the digestive system—the liver and the pancreas—both of which connect to the small intestine. It is from these two organs that many of the essential digestive juices are secreted. The function of the digestive system is to change the composition of foods ingested. Reduced to simpler chemical substances, the food can be readily absorbed through the lining of the intestines for distribution by the circulatory system to the millions of body cells. These end products of digestion are in the form of simple sugars, fatty acids, amino acids, minerals, and vitamins.

Digestion is also accomplished by mechanical action. First, the food is broken down by the grinding action of the teeth. This increases the food surface area upon which the various digestive juices can act. Food is then swallowed and eventually is moved through the alimentary canal by a process called *peristalsis*. This is a series of muscular contractions that mixes the content of the digestive tract and keeps it moving.

The digestive tract is exceedingly responsive to a person's emotional state. Food eaten under happy conditions tends to be readily digested. On the contrary, digestion may be impeded and even stopped for a considerable period of time (as much as a day or more) if severe emotional stress occurs. Extensive nerve connections in the digestive tract tend to make its organs especially susceptible to disorders caused by emotional disturbance. Examples of some of these disorders are nausea, diarrhea, and colitis (inflammation of the large bowel). In such disorders the organs involved may not necessarily be diseased; there may only be impaired functioning of the organ. However, many authorities agree that prolonged emotional stress can lead to serious diseases of the digestive tract.

Some believe that a bowel movement per day is essential to health, and that to be really effective this movement should occur at the same time each day. If not, they believe autointoxication, or self-poisoning, may result. Many people do find a bowel movement once a day satisfactory and having it at a particular time, convenient. However, just as some require more than one elimination per day, others find every other day a natural rhythm—and not a cause of constipation. Thus, the problem is not one of conforming to an arbitrary standard, but discovering a natural rhythm and responding to the urge when it comes.

Various things commonly interrupt bowel rhythm. For example, altering a customary routine, rising at a different hour, failing to exercise, and failing to eat enough food containing fiber, which normally stimulates peristaltic action. The resulting feeling of discomfort, headache, or irritability ("constipation symptoms"), do not necessarily result from self-poisoning or autointoxication caused by fecal matter reentering the blood stream. It seems likely that the emphasis that many parents put on "moving the bowels" leads many people to overexaggerate the importance of failing to do so on schedule. Generally speaking, the individual who has a good diet including adequate fluids, and is active, can trust his or her body to tend to itself in its automatic function. Presupposing a generally healthful pattern of living, perhaps patience rather than grim concern and laxatives is the reasonable prescription. Needless to say, a physician should be consulted in the event of marked or prolonged deviation from normal bowel-moving behavior.

Diet

The term *diet* is an all-inclusive one used to refer to foods and liquids regularly consumed. The question often raised is, What consti-

tutes a balanced diet? This means essentially that along with sufficient fluids, one should include foods from the four basic food
groups. These are the dairy group, the meat group, the vegetable and
fruit group, and the bread and cereal group.

A guide to a balanced diet was prepared by the staff of the United
States Senate Select Committee on Nutrition and Human Needs. This
committee spent a great deal of time on hearings and research, and
some of its recommendations are listed as follows.

1. Eat less meat and more fish and poultry.
2. Replace whole milk with skim milk.
3. Reduce intake of eggs, butter, and other high-cholesterol sources.
4. Cut back on sugars to 15 percent of daily caloric intake.
5. Reduce intake of salt to a total of three grams a day.
6. Eat more fruit, vegetables, and whole grain.

These recommendations are directed to the general population.
However, one important factor must be noted, and this is that eating is
an individual matter. The problem may not be so much one of following an arbitrary diet, but one of learning to know on what foods and
proportions of foods one functions best. The body is capable of com-
pensating for an imbalance in nutrients that we fail to get if the short-
age is made up within a reasonable period of time. In other words, it is
not necessary to have an exactly balanced diet at every meal. Indeed,
it is possible to miss meals—even go for several days without food—
and show no signs of malnutrition. The important consideration seems
to be in the quality of the total intake over periods of time.

The foregoing observations should not be interpreted to mean that
one should be indifferent or careless about food choices. After all, literally, we are what we eat. It is absurd that some people are more
careful about what they feed their pets than about what they feed
themselves.

Eating Habits of Children

Adult supervision, especially that of parents, is of utmost importance in children's eating habits. However, in some cases parents may
be the child's worst enemy as far as eating habits are concerned. The

nagging parent who tries to ply the child with food that he or she may not like and the constant admonishment of "clean your plate" oftentimes can do a great deal of harm to the child's present and future eating habits.

The diets of some families include too much of certain foods that can be potentially harmful to the adult members as well to its children. A case in point is the intake of cholesterol. Excessive amounts of this chemical component of animal oils and fats are deposited in blood vessels and may be a factor in the hardening of the arteries leading to a heart attack.

In *The Healing Heart,* Norman Cousins suggests that the accumulation of these fatty substances is not something that begins in middle age. On the contrary, the process can begin in early childhood. Cousins reports on a study of children in New York City and Los Angeles by the American Heart Foundation that showed average cholesterol levels of 180 for children in the ten- to twelve-year-old age range. Continuing on this same course would lead to cholesterol levels close to or above 300 by age thirty-five.[2]

Physicians vary widely in their beliefs about safe levels of cholesterol and not long ago a very broad range of 150 to 300 was considered normal. However, recent thoughts on this matter have changed radically. For example, the National Heart, Lung, and Blood Institute has announced more stringent guidelines. That is, it is now believed that total blood cholesterol should not go over 200 (this means 200 milligrams (mg) of total cholesterol per deciliter (dl) of blood). In this general regard it is interesting that the National Cholesterol Education Program suggests the following intake for children as compared to adults.

	Children	*Adults*
Acceptable	Less than 170 mg/dl	Less than 200 mg/dl
Borderline	170 to 199 mg/dl	200 to 239 mg/dl
High	Above 200 mg/dl	Above 240 mg/dl[3]

By age one, children begin to have a rather remarkable change in their eating habits. For one thing, there is likely to be a large decrease in the intake of food. Many parents who do not understand the process of child growth and development worry needlessly about this. What actually happens is that after the first year the growth rate of the child declines and as a consequence the need for calories per pound of body weight becomes less. This causes the appetite to decrease, and this can vary from one meal to another, sometimes depending upon the kind and amount of activity in which the child engages. Thus, a parent who is aware of this will not expect the child of two or three years of age to eat the way he or she did at six months. This knowledge for the parent is very important because then he or she will not be so concerned with the *quantity* of the child's intake of food. This is to say that parents should be more concerned with the *quality* of food than the amount of intake.

Children may develop a sudden like or dislike for certain foods. Reasons vary for this change in attitude. They may want a particular cereal because of the prize in the box, and then may turn the food down because they are disenchanted and do not want the prize. Fortunately, more often than not, such likes and dislikes are not long-lasting, and adults should not worry too much about them.

It is a good practice to provide a large variety of foods early in the child's life. This helps to prevent him or her from forming set opinions on food likes and dislikes. Adults should set an example by not allowing their own dislikes to influence children.

Adults often complain that a child is a "poor eater." When this occurs it is important to try to identify the cause of this problem. It may be that the child too frequently eats alone and is deprived of the pleasant company of others. Or perhaps the portions are too large, particularly if the child feels that he or she must consume all of the food on the plate. Mealtime should be a happy time. It is not a time for reprimanding and threatening if a child does not eat heartily. Such behavior on the part of adults can place the child under stress and create an eating problem that otherwise would probably not occur.

In my studies of nine- to ten-year-old children I found that generally they were aware of foods that were *best* for health and those that were *worst* for health. Those foods identified as best were: vegetables, 36 percent; fruits, 28 percent; meat, 26 percent; bread, 8 percent; and somewhat surprisingly, milk, only 2 percent. As for the worst foods for health: 65 percent said candy and other sweets; 17 percent said junk foods; 9 percent said salt; 5 percent said coffee; and 4 percent said fats.

In one interesting study, ten- to eleven-year-olds were asked to name their favorite foods. The results in order of preference: pizza, hamburgers, spaghetti, ice cream, hot dogs, popcorn, and brownies.[4] Of course these results should not be misinterpreted to suggest that these foods consist of a child's regular diet, but rather that they are the foods the children tend to like best. Nonetheless, a disturbing estimate is that Americans eat as many as one-half of their meals out, and that these out-of-home meals are likely to be from fast-food establishments.

Rest and Sleep

To be effective in life pursuits, periodic recuperation is an essential ingredient in daily living patterns. Rest and sleep provide us with the means of revitalizing ourselves to meet the challenges of our responsibilities. In order to keep fatigue at a minimum and in its proper proportion in the cycle of everyday activities, nature has provided us with ways that help combat and reduce it.

There are two types of fatigue, *acute* and *chronic*. Acute fatigue is a natural outcome of sustained severe exertion. It is due to physical factors, such as the accumulation of the by-products of muscular exertion in the blood, and to excessive oxygen debt—the ability of the body to take in as much oxygen as is being consumed by muscular work. Psychological considerations may also be important in acute fatigue. Individuals who are bored with their work and who become preoccupied with the discomfort involved will become fatigued much sooner than if they are highly motivated to do the same work, but are not bored, and do not think about the discomfort.

Chronic fatigue refers to fatigue that lasts over extended periods, in contrast to acute fatigue, which tends to be followed by a recovery phase and restoration to "normal" within a more or less brief period of time. Chronic fatigue may be due to any or a variety of medical conditions ranging from disease to malnutrition. (Such conditions are the concern of the physician, who should evaluate all cases of chronic fatigue in order to ensure that a disease condition is not responsible.)

Rest and sleep are essential to life as they afford the body the chance to regain its vitality and efficiency in a very positive way. Learning to utilize opportunities for rest and sleep may add years to our lives and zest to our years. Although rest and sleep are closely allied, they are not synonymous and should be considered separately.

Rest

Most people think of rest as just "taking it easy." The purpose of rest is to reduce tension so that the body may be better able to recover from fatigue. There is no overt activity involved, but neither is there loss of consciousness, as in sleep. In rest, there is no loss of awareness of the external environment as there is in sleep. Since the need for rest is usually in direct proportion to the type of activity in which we engage, it follows naturally that the more strenuous the activity, the more frequent the rest periods should be. A busy day at school may not be as noticeably active as a game of tennis; nevertheless, it is the wise person who will let the body dictate when a rest period is required. Five or ten minutes of sitting in a chair with eyes closed may make the difference in the course of an active day, assuming of course that this is possible. The real effectiveness of rest periods depends largely upon the individual and his or her ability to sit down and rest.

Sleep

Sleep is a phenomenon that has never been clearly defined or understood, but it has aptly been described as the "great restorer." It is no wonder that authorities on the subject agree that sleep is essential to the vital functioning of the body and that natural sleep is the most satisfying form of recuperation from fatigue. It is during the hours of sleep that the body is given the opportunity to revitalize itself. All vital functions are slowed down so that the building of new cells and the repair of tissues can take place without undue interruption. This does not mean that the body builds and regenerates tissue only during sleep, but it does mean that it is the time that nature has set aside to accomplish the task more easily. The body's metabolic rate is lowered and energy is restored.

Despite the acknowledged need for sleep, a question of paramount importance concerns the amount necessary for the body to accomplish its recuperative task. There is no clear-cut answer to this query. Sleep is an individual matter. The usual recommendation for adults is eight hours of sleep out of every twenty-four, but the basis for this could well be one of fallacy rather than fact. Many people can function effectively on less sleep, and others require more. No matter how many hours of sleep a person gets during the course of a twenty-four-hour period, the best test of adequacy will depend largely on how he or she feels. If the person is alert, feels healthy, and is in good humor, he or she is probably getting a sufficient amount of sleep. The rest that sleep normally brings to the body depends upon a person's freedom from excessive emotional tension and ability to relax. Unrelaxed sleep has little restorative value.

Is loss of sleep dangerous? Again, the answer is not simple. To the healthy person with normal sleep habits, occasionally missing the accustomed hours of sleep is not serious. Under normal conditions, a night of lost sleep followed by a period of prolonged sleep will restore the individual to his or her normal self. However, repeated loss of sleep over a period of time can be dangerous. Loss of sleep night after night, rather than at one time, can result in poor general health, nervousness, irritability, inability to concentrate, lowered perseverance of effort, and chronic fatigue. Studies have shown that a person can go for much longer periods of time without food than without sleep.

Many conditions can rob the body of restful slumber. Most certainly, mental anguish and worry play a very large part in holding sleep at bay. Other factors that influence the quality of sleep are hunger, cold, boredom, and excessive fatigue. Insomnia and chronic fatigue should be brought to the attention of a physician so that the necessary steps can be taken to bring about restoration of normal sleep patterns. Certainly, drugs to induce sleep should be utilized only if prescribed by a physician.

Some recommendations about sleep might include the following: (1) relaxing physically and mentally before retiring; (2) reducing tension levels during the day; (3) managing time, activities, and thoughts to prepare for a good night's sleep; and (4) beginning the process at the same time each night, doing the same things, leading to repose at the same hour. That is, if a person's bedtime is normally 11:00 p.m., preparation should perhaps begin at least by 10:00 p.m. and probably not later than 10:30 p.m.

Sleeping Habits of Children

During the first year of a child's life it is common practice to have two nap periods, one in the morning and one in the afternoon. The year-old child gradually gives up the morning nap and this tends to increase afternoon nap time as well as night sleep. With age the child will decrease the afternoon nap time and, as a consequence, he or she will sleep longer at night. Although there is some difference of opinion on when children should give up both the morning and afternoon nap, preschoolers should have at least one nap a day, preferably in the afternoon.

As in the case of adults, school-age children differ in the number of hours of sleep required. The general recommendation is that on average out of every twenty-four hours they should get at least nine hours of sleep. A very important factor is that bedtime should be a happy time. Adults should not make such an issue of it that conflict results. Perhaps a good rule for a younger child is that he or she be "taken" to bed rather than "sent." The ritual of reading or telling the child a pleasant story at bedtime is important and can help lessen the impact of sudden separation. It is important to remember that some of the sleep disorders of young children can be traced directly to stressful conditions under which separation at bedtime occurs. It is interesting to note that research reported at the National Academy of Science in September 1999 indicated that the circadian rhythms of teenagers are geared toward a later sleep time and a later waking time than for adults or younger children.[5] This has caused some school districts to start school forty-five minutes to one hour later than has been customary.

It is important to remember that understanding the complex nature of sleep may be the province of scientists and other qualified experts, but an understanding of the value of sleep is the responsibility of everyone.

Physical Activity and Exercise

When used in connection with the human organism, the term *physical* means a concern for the body and its needs. The term *activity* derives from the word "active," one meaning of which is the requirement of action. Thus, physical activity implies body action. This is a broad term and could include any voluntary and/or involuntary body movement. When such body movement is practiced for the purpose of developing and maintaining physical fitness, it is ordinarily referred to as physical exercise.

Physical Activity for Children

One of the most important characteristics of life is movement. Practically all of our achievements are based on our ability to move. Very young children are not capable of abstract thinking, and they only gradually acquire the ability to deal with symbols and intellectualize their experiences in the course of development. Any effort to help them grow, develop, learn, and be reasonably free from stress and tension must take this dominance of movement into account.

Most children—unless there is a serious impairment—will engage in physical activity if given the opportunity to do so. They run, jump, climb, and play games requiring these movement skills. Some adults consider this so-called "free play" meaningless. On the contrary, it is very meaningful to children as they explore various ways to move their bodies through space. In addition to this unorganized form of activity various types of organized physical activity programs are available for children. In general, these can be classified into (1) school programs, and (2) out-of-school programs.

School programs. Most elementary schools try to provide a well-balanced physical education program for students. Just as young children need to learn the basic skills of reading, writing, and mathematics, they should also learn basic physical skills.

For young children, being able to move as effectively and efficiently as possible is directly related to the proficiency with which they will be able to perform various fundamental physical skills. In turn, the success that children have in sports activities requiring certain motor skills will be dependent upon their proficiency of performance of these skills. Thus, effective and efficient movement is prerequisite to the performance of basic motor skills needed for success in school physical education activities. These activities include active games, rhythmic activities, and gymnastics.

Out-of-school programs. Out-of-school programs are provided by various organizations such as boys' and girls' clubs and neighborhood recreation centers. These programs vary in quality depending upon the extent of suitable facilities and qualified personnel available to supervise and conduct them. Parents should investigate these programs thoroughly to make sure they are designed in the best interests of the children. This is mentioned because some highly competitive sports programs for children place more emphasis on adult pride than

on the welfare of children. This should not be interpreted as an indict-
ment against all out-of-school programs, because many of them do a
commendable job.

Some families do not rely on any kind of organized out-of-school
program, preferring instead to plan their own. This is an excellent idea
because it can make for fine family relationships as well as provide
wholesome physical activity for the entire family. There is much truth
in the old adage: "The family that plays together stays together."

Chapter 3

Stress As a Factor
in Child Development

CHILDREN AND STRESS

Although we tend to associate stress with adults, it can have a devastating effect on developing children as well. In fact, stress can take a tremendous toll on their physical, social, emotional, and intellectual development.

As children enter the various stages of development, many are beset with problems of stress. The first stage of child development, occurring from birth to about fifteen months, is considered to be the "intake" stage, because behavior and growth during this period are characterized by *taking in*. This applies not only to food but to other things, such as sound, light, and the various forms of care received. At this early stage in the child's life separation anxiety can begin. Since the child is entirely dependent on the mother or other caregiver to meet his or her needs, separation may be seen as being deprived of these important needs. It is at this stage that the child's caregiver—ordinarily the parent—should try to maintain a proper balance between meeting the child's needs and overgratification. Many child development experts agree that children who experience some stress from separation or from having to wait for a need to be fulfilled gain the opportunity to organize their psychological resources and adapt to stress. On the contrary, children who did not have this balance may tend to disorganize under stress.

During the stage from about fifteen months to three years, children develop autonomy. This can be described as the "I am what I can do" stage. Autonomy develops because most children can now move about rather easily. The child does not have to rely entirely on a caregiver to meet every single need. Autonomy also results from the development of mental processes, because the child can think about things and put language to use.

Toilet training can be a major stressor during this stage. Children are not always given the needed opportunity to express autonomy during this process. It can be a difficult time for them, because they are ordinarily expected to cooperate with, and gain the approval of, caregivers. If children cooperate and use the toilet, approval is forthcoming; however, some autonomy is lost. If they do not cooperate, disapproval may result. If the conflict is not resolved satisfactorily, some clinical psychologists believe it will emerge during adulthood in the form of highly anxious and compulsive behaviors.

The next stage, from three to five years, can be described as "I am what I think I am." Skills of body movement are being used in a more purposeful way. Children develop the ability to daydream and make believe, and these are used to manifest some of their behaviors. Pretending allows them to be whatever they want to be—anything from astronauts to zebras. It is possible, however, that resorting to too much fantasy may result in stress, because some children may become scared of their own fantasies. Unquestionably, children at all age levels are likely to encounter a considerable amount of stress. The objectives of those adults who work with children should be to help them reduce stress by making a change in the environment and/or helping the children to make a change in themselves.

Each person has a tolerance level as far as stress is concerned. If the stress becomes considerably greater than the tolerance, a person will suffer from emotional stress and its negative consequences. Indeed, the average child's environment abounds with many stress-inducing factors—society in general, home, and school. Factors such as adult behavior can also have a frustrating influence on children.

Adults who work with children should have an understanding of the stress concept as well as the stress placed on children in their various environments. Under certain conditions sports can be stressful for children, especially if they are pressured to win. Adults who have an awareness of this are in a better position to help children avoid stress and to cope with it when it does occur.

Not all problems concerned with childhood stress are evident in the adult population, however. One such problem is that children are not as likely to be able to successfully cope with stress. The following are some options for coping with stress that are open to adults, but not to children.

1. An open display of anger is often considered unacceptable for children. For example, a teacher can be angry with a student, but children may not have the same right to be angry with a teacher.
2. Adults have the latitude of withdrawing or walking out, but this same option of freedom may not be available to children.
3. Some child psychologists believe that daydreaming is therapeutic and productive. At the same time, children may be reprimanded for "daydreaming" in school.

As a result, it is possible that children may be punished for using the same kinds of coping behaviors and techniques that are satisfactory for adults. Some of these behaviors are considered socially unacceptable for children.

THE MEANING OF STRESS

No solid agreement has been reached regarding the derivation of the term *stress*. Some sources suggest that the term is derived from the Latin word *stringere,* meaning to "bind tightly." Other sources contend that the term derives from the French word *destress* (in English: *distress*), and suggest that the prefix "dis" was eventually eliminated because of slurring, as in the case of the word *because* sometimes becoming *'cause*.

A generalized description of the term is a "constraining force or influence." When applied to human beings, this could be interpreted to mean the extent to which the body can withstand a given force or influence. In this regard one of the most often quoted descriptions of stress is that of Hans Selye, who described it as the "nonspecific response of the body to any demand made upon it."[1]

Selye's definition means that stress involves a mobilization of bodily resources in response to some sort of stimulus (stressor). These responses can include various physical and chemical changes in the body. This description of stress could be extended by saying that it involves demands that tax and/or exceed the resources of the human body. This means that stress involves not only these bodily responses but also the wear and tear on the body brought about by these responses. In essence, stress can be considered as any factor acting internally or externally which makes it difficult to adapt and which induces increased effort on the part of individuals to maintain a state of balance within themselves and the external environment. It should be understood that stress is a state that individuals are in, and this should not be confused with any stimuli that produce such a state (stressors).

THE STRESS CONCEPT

Although there are various theories of stress, one of the basic and better-known ones is that of the previously mentioned Hans Selye. The physiological processes and the reactions involved in Selye's stress model are identified as the general adaptation syndrome and consist of three stages: alarm reaction, resistance, and exhaustion.

In alarm reaction, the body reacts to the stressor and causes the hypothalamus to produce a biochemical "messenger," which in turn causes the pituitary to secrete ACTH into the bloodstream.[2] This hormone then causes the adrenals to discharge adrenaline and other corticoids. This causes shrinkage of the thymus with an influence on heart rate, blood pressure, etc. It is during alarm reaction that the resistance of the body is reduced.

Resistance develops if the stressor is not too pronounced, body adaptation develops to fight back the stress or possibly to avoid it, and the body begins to repair any damage.

Exhaustion occurs if there is continuous exposure to the same stressor. The ability of adaptation is eventually exhausted and the signs of alarm reaction reappear. Selye contends that our adaptation resources are limited, and when they become irreversible, the result is death. (We should all keep our resistance and capacity for adaptation.)

HOME STRESS

Changes in society with consequent changes in the conditions in some homes are likely to make adjustment a difficult problem for children. Such factors as changes in standards of female behavior, larger percentages of both parents working, economic conditions, mass media such as television, and numerous others can complicate their lives.

Child psychiatrists are convinced that some home conditions can have an extremely negative influence on the personality and mental health of some children, not only at their present stage of development but in the future as well. In fact, studies show that the interaction of stress factors is especially important. These studies identified the following factors to be strongly associated with childhood (and possibly later) psychiatric disorders:

1. Severe marital discord
2. Low social status
3. Overcrowding or large family size
4. Paternal criminality
5. Maternal psychiatric disorder
6. Admission into the care of local authorities

It is estimated that, with only one of these conditions present, a child is no more likely to develop psychiatric problems than any other child. However, when two of the conditions occur, the child's psychiatric risk increases fourfold.

My own surveys found that certain actions of parents induced stress in teachers and, according to the teachers, these parental attitudes might well be considered as stress-inducing factors for their students. These actions can be classified into three areas: (1) lack of concern of parents for their children, (2) parental interference, and (3) lack of parental support for teachers.

In almost half of the cases, lack of parental concern for children was stressful for teachers. They cited such issues as parents not caring when a student did poorly, parents not willing to help their children with schoolwork, a lack of home discipline, and stress placed on teachers by the difficulty they had getting parents to attend conferences.

About one-third of the teachers said parental interference was often a result of having unrealistic expectations of their children; this in turn resulted in parental pressure on children, particularly for grades, which may be one of the most serious conditions in schools today— from kindergarten through the university level.

The third classification of parental actions causing stress for teachers is lack of parental support, and slightly less than 25 percent have identified stress-inducing factors. They were stressed by such factors as not being supported by parents and a general poor attitude of parents toward teachers.

Another important home condition that can induce stress in children is when the family itself is under stress. Parenting is an extremely difficult task and the demands of it are becoming more and more complicated. Consequently, many of the pressures that modern parents are called upon to endure not only cause stress for them but also cause them to induce stress upon their children as well.

It has been estimated that over one million children are abused or neglected by their parents or other "overseers" in our country annually, and that as many as 2,000 die as a result of maltreatment. Authorities suggest that most of this is not caused by inhuman, hateful intent on the part of parents, but rather it is the result of a combination of factors, including both the accumulation of stresses on families and the parents' unmet needs for support in coping with their child-rearing responsibilities.[3]

SCHOOL STRESS

A number of conditions exist in many school situations that can cause stress for children. These conditions prevail at all levels—possibly in different ways—from the time a child enters school until graduation from college.

School Anxiety

School anxiety as a child stressor is a phenomenon with which educators, particularly teachers, frequently find themselves confronted in their dealing with children. Various theories have been advanced to explain this phenomenon and relate it to other character traits and emotional dispositions. Literature on the subject reveals the following characteristics of anxiety as a stress-inducing factor in the educative process.

1. Anxiety is considered a learnable reaction that has the properties of a response, a cue of danger, and a drive.

2. Anxiety is internalized fear aroused by the memory of painful past experiences associated with a punishment for the gratification of an impulse.
3. Anxiety in the classroom interferes with learning, and whatever can be done to reduce it should serve as a spur to learning.
4. Test anxiety is a near-universal experience, especially in this country which is a test-giving and test-conscious culture.
5. Evidence from clinical studies points clearly and consistently to the disruptive and distracting effect of anxiety over most kinds of thinking.

It would seem that causes of anxiety change with age as do perceptions of stressful situations. Care should be taken in assessing the total life space of the child—background, home life, school life, age, and gender—in order to minimize the anxiety experienced in the school. School anxiety, although manifested in the school environment, may often be caused by unrelated factors outside the school.

Separation Anxiety

One of the most stressful life events for young children is starting school. One of the reasons for this may possibly be that older childhood friends, siblings, and even some unthinking parents admonish the child with, "Wait until you get to school—you're going to get it." This kind of negative attitude is likely to increase any separation anxiety that the child already has.

As mentioned previously, separation anxiety begins in the first stage of the child's development, from birth to about fifteen months. It can reach a peak in the latter part of the developmental stage, from three to five years, because it is the first attempt to become a part of the outer world—at school. For many children this is the first task of enforced separation. For those who do not have a well-developed sense of continuity, the separation might easily be equated with the loss of the life-sustaining mother. The stress associated with such a disaster could be overwhelming for such a child. Learning to tolerate the stress of separation is one of the central concerns of preschoolers; adults should be alert to signs and seek to lessen the impact. Compromises should be made not necessarily to remove the stress but to help the child gradually build a tolerance for separation.

In extreme cases of the separation problem, a child's reaction may typically include temper tantrums, crying, screaming, and downright refusal to go to school. Or, in some cases, suspiciously sudden aches and pains might serve to keep the "sick" child home. What the child is reacting against is not the school but separation from the mother. The stress associated with this event may be seen by the child as a devastating loss equated with being abandoned. The child's behavior in dealing with the stress can be so extreme as to demand special treatment on the part of the significant adults in his or her life.

The aim in such cases should always be to ease the transition into school. It is important to keep in mind that separation is a two-way street. Assuring parents of the competence of the school staff and the physical safety of their child may go a long way toward helping to reduce the stress. If adults act responsibly and consistently, the child should be able to make an adequate adjustment to this daily separation from family and, in the process, learn an important lesson in meeting reality demands.

Curriculum

Various school subjects areas could be considered as perennial nemeses for many students. Probably any subject could induce stress for certain students. Prominent among those stressful subjects are those concerned with the three Rs. For example, for many children, attending school daily and performing poorly is a source of considerable and prolonged stress. If they overreact to environmental stresses in terms of increased muscle tension, it may interfere with the fluid muscular movement required in handwriting tasks. They may press hard on their paper, purse their lips, and tighten their bodies, using an inordinate amount of energy and concentration to write while performing at a very low level.

Reading is another area of school activity that is loaded with anxiety, stress, and frustration for many children. In fact, one of the levels of reading recognized by reading specialists is called the "frustration level." In terms of behavioral observation this can be described as the level in which children show tension, excessive or erratic body movements, nervousness, and distractibility. This frustration level is said to be a sign of emotional tension or stress with breakdowns in fluency and a significant increase in reading errors.

A study by Swain determined the extent to which stress was a factor in primary schoolchildren's reading difficulties.[4] She investigated referral and evaluation statements and diagnostic data from parents, teachers, reading specialists, and counselors regarding signs of stress as potential factors in the reading difficulties of seventy-seven primary schoolchildren referred for evaluation at the Pupil Appraisal Center (PAC) at North Texas State University between 1977 and 1984.

Situational analysis was employed to obtain a holistic view of each child's reading difficulties. The researcher collected data from documented files at PAC. Data analysis via a categorical coding system produced thirty-nine stress-related categories, organized under broad headings of family and school environment, readiness for reading/learning, general stress reactions, and responses to stress when reading/learning becomes a problem.

The most significant signs of stress cited in this study were symptoms of anxiety and a marked tendency toward passivity and unassertiveness. Primary potential stressors also emerged. Intellectual and language deficits were noted, along with self-defeating behaviors, absence of self-motivation/self-control, and problems stemming from the home and school environment.

Support for findings in referral and evaluation statements was found in diagnostic data that included intelligence, reading, and projective tests. Some of the children had specific personal limitations that might have hindered reading. However, many were experiencing frustrations from working at capacity and yet not meeting parental or teacher expectations. No child was found to be coping effectively with apparent adverse circumstances. Failure by many of these children to adapt successfully to stress in their personal lives could forecast chronic difficulty in reading when it, too, becomes a challenge to them.

The subject that appears to stress the greatest majority of students is mathematics. In fact, this has become such a problem in recent years that there is now an area of study called "math anxiety" that is receiving increasing attention. "Math anxious" and "math avoiding" people tend not to trust their problem-solving abilities and experience a high level of stress when asked to use them. Even though these people are not necessarily "mathematically ignorant," they tend to feel that they are, simply because they cannot focus on the problem at hand or because they are unable to remember the appropriate formulas. Thus, a feeling of frustration and incompetence is likely to make them reluctant to deal with mathematics in their daily lives. It is suggested that at the root of this self-doubt is a fear of making mistakes and appearing stupid in front of others.

It is believed that at least three sources of anxiety are commonly found in traditional mathematics classes: (1) time pressure, (2) humiliation, and (3) emphasis on one right answer. As far as time pressure is concerned, such tools as flash cards, timed tests, and competition in which the object is to finish first are among the first experiences that can make lasting negative impressions. Slower learners are soon likely to become apprehensive when asked to perform a mathematics problem.

One of the strongest memories of some math-anxious adults is the feeling of humiliation at being called upon to perform in front of the class. As children, they were asked to go to the chalkboard to struggle over a problem until a solution was found. If an error was made, the individual was prodded to locate and correct it. In this kind of stressful situation, it is not surprising that children are likely to experience "math block," which adds to the sense of humiliation and failure. This should not be interpreted to mean that the chalkboard should not be used creatively to demonstrate problem-solving abilities. A child who successfully performs a mathematical task in front of classmates can have the enjoyable experience of instructing others. Also, the rest of the class can gain useful information from watching how another solves a problem. When using chalkboard practice, however, it is important to remember that children profit from demonstrating their competence and not their weaknesses.

Although mathematics problems do, in most cases, have correct answers, it can be a mistake to focus only on accuracy. In putting too much emphasis on the end product, oftentimes overlooked is the valuable information about the process involved in arriving at that product. Teachers should reward creative thinking as well as correct answers. Again, the reader should not interpret this as meaning that the correct answer is not important. However, when it is emphasized to the exclusion of all other information, students can become fearful of making mistakes and possibly angry with themselves when they do.

Tests

In more than forty years as a teacher—which included all levels from elementary school through the graduate level—I have observed many students who were seriously stressed by "testphobia," or what is more commonly known as *test anxiety.*

Two prominent authorities on the subject, Bernard Brown and Lilian Rosenbaum, contend that perceived stress appears to depend on psychological sets and responses that individuals are more likely to bring into the testing situation than manufacture on the spot. Students respond to tests and testing situations with learned patterns of stress reactivity. The patterns may vary among individuals and may reflect differences in autonomic nervous system conditioning, feelings of threat or worry regarding the symbolic meaning of the test or the testing situation, and coping skills that govern the management of complexity, frustration, information load, symbolic manipulation, and mobilization of resources. There are also individual patterns of maladaptive behavior such as anxiety, a sustained level of autonomic activity after exposure to a stressor, and the use of a variety of such defense mechanisms as learned helplessness and avoidance behavior.[5]

Perceived stress also depends upon the nature of the task to be performed. As tasks get more complex and require greater degrees of coordination and integration of the nervous system, a given stressor level will affect task performance as if it were a stronger stressor.

What then does the nature of test anxiety imply for educational goals and practices? Perhaps there should be a continuing opportunity for all school personnel and parents to report on their experiences with the tests that have been used. This feedback should also place a great deal of emphasis on the students' reactions to their testing experiences. It is essential that the reactions of children that give evidence of emotional disturbance in regard to tests be carefully considered, especially when test results are interpreted and used for instructional guidance and administrative purposes.

Finally, it is important to take a positive attitude when considering test results. That is, emphasis should be placed on the number of answers that were correct: "You got seven right," rather than "You missed three." It has been my experience that this approach can help minimize future test-taking stress.

Gender Differences

In general, emotional stress seems to have a greater effect on boys than on girls in both the school and home environments. One possible exception to this in the school situation is that girls are prone to suffer more anxiety over report cards than are boys. Most studies show that boys are much more likely to be stressed by family discord and disruption than are girls, although there does not seem to be a completely satisfactory explanation for this.

Many people have been critical of the early school learning environment, particularly where boys are concerned. They have gone so far as to say that young boys are discriminated against in their early school years. Let us examine the premise.

A generally accepted description of learning is that it involves some sort of change in behavior. Many learning theorists agree that behavior is a product of heredity and environment. Unquestionably, it is apparent that environment plays a major role in determining a person's behavior, and some tend to feel that man is, indeed, controlled by his environment. Nevertheless, we must remember that it is an environment largely of his own making. The issue here is whether or not an environment is provided that is best suited for boys at the early age levels, and further whether such an environment is likely to cause more stress among young boys than young girls.

Although the school has no control over ancestry, it can, within certain limitations, exercise some degree of control over the kind of environment in which the learner must function. Generally speaking, it is doubtful that all schools have provided an environment that is most conducive to learning as far as young boys are concerned. Many child development specialists have characterized the environment at the elementary school level of education as *feminized*. A major factor to consider concerns the biological differences between boys and girls in this particular age range, and it may be questionable whether educational planning has always taken these important differences into account. Over the years there has been an accumulation of evidence on the general subject appearing in the literature on child development, some of which is summarized here.

Due to certain hormonal conditions, boys tend to be more aggressive, restless, and impatient. In addition, the male has more rugged bone structure and, as a consequence, greater strength than the female at all ages. Because of this, males tend to display greater muscular re-activity that in turn expresses itself in a stronger tendency toward restlessness and vigorous overt activity. This condition is concerned with the greater oxygen consumption required to fulfill the male's need for increased energy production. The male organism might be compared to an engine that operates at higher levels of speed and intensity than the less energetic female organism.

Another factor to take into account is the difference in basal metabolic rate (BMR) in young boys and young girls. The BMR is indicative of the speed at which body fuel is changed into energy, as well as how fast this energy is used. The BMR can be measured in terms of calories per meter of body surface with a calorie representing a unit measure of heat energy in food. It has been found, on average, BMR rises from birth to about three years of age and then starts to decline until the ages of approximately twenty to twenty-four. The BMR is higher for boys than for girls, particularly at the early age levels. Because of the higher BMR, boys in turn will have a higher amount of energy to expend. Because of differences in sex hormonal conditions and BMR, it appears logical that these factors will influence the male in his behavior patterns.

From a growth and developmental point of view, although at birth the female is from one-half to one centimeter less in length than the male and around 300 grams less in weight, she is perhaps actually a much better developed organism. It is estimated on the average that at the time of entrance into school, the female is usually six to twelve months more physically mature than the male. As a result, girls may be likely to learn earlier how to perform tasks of manual dexterity, such as buttoning their clothing. In one of my own observational studies of preschool children, I found that little girls were able to perform the task of tying their shoelaces at a rate of almost four times that of little boys.

Although all schools should not be categorized in the same manner, some of them have been captured by tradition and ordinarily provide an environment that places emphasis upon such factors as neatness, orderliness, and passiveness, which are easier for girls to conform to than boys. Of course, this may be partly because our culture tends to force females to be identified with many of these characteristics.

The authoritarian and sedentary classroom atmosphere that prevails in some schools, which involves only the "sit still and listen" learning method, fails to take into account the greater activity drive and physical aggressiveness of boys. What have been characterized as feminization traits prevail in some elementary schools and tend to have an adverse influence on the young male child as far as learning is concerned.

Some studies have shown that as far as hyperactivity is concerned, hyperactive boys may outnumber girls by a ratio of as much as nine to one. This may be one of the reasons that teachers generally tend to rate young males as being so much more aggressive than females, with the result that young boys are considered to be more negative and extroverted. Because of these characteristics, boys generally have poorer relationships with their teachers than do girls, and in the area of behavior problems and discipline in the age range from five to eight years, boys account for twice as many disturbances as girls. The importance of this factor is borne out when it is considered that good teacher-pupil relationships tend to raise the achievement levels of both sexes.

Various studies have shown that girls generally receive higher grades than boys, although boys may achieve as well as, and in some instances, better than girls. It is also clearly evident that boys in the early years fail twice as often as girls, even when there is no significant difference between intelligence and achievement test scores of both sexes. This suggests that even though both sexes have the same intellectual tools, other factors militate against learning as far as boys are concerned.

If a person is willing to accept the research findings and observational evidence appearing in the child development literature regarding this outlined premise, the question is, What attempts, if any, are being made to improve the condition? At one time it was thought that the solution might lie in defeminization of the schools at the early age levels by putting more men into classrooms. This apparently met with little success because the learning environment remains essentially the same regardless of the teacher's gender. Some educators have suggested that young boys should start school later or that little girls start earlier. The problem with this, of course, is that state laws concerned with school entrance are likely to distinguish only in terms of age and not gender. In a few remote instances, some schools have experimented with separating boys and girls at the early grade levels. This method of grouping resulted in both groups achieving at a higher level than when the sexes were in classes together in some cases.

What can be done to at least partially restructure an environment that will be more favorable to the learning of young boys? One step in this direction, recommended by various child development specialists, is to develop curriculum content that is more *action* oriented, thus taking into account the basic need for motor activity involved in human learning. This is to say that deep consideration might well be given to learning activities through which excess energy, especially of boys, could be utilized.

Several causes and contributing causes of stress have been dealt with in the preceding discussions. It is possible to eliminate many of these stress-inducing factors. For those which cannot be eliminated entirely, serious attempts should be made to at least keep them under control if we are to succeed in providing for total development of children.

Chapter 4

An Overview of Children's Sports

Children's sports, here defined as the organized interactions of children in competitive and/or cooperative team or individual enjoyable physical activities, have reached almost unbelievable proportions of growth today. Using Little League baseball as an example, there are probably some three million participants on more than 180,000 teams in over sixty countries. In addition, more than 750,000 volunteers worldwide participate in this program.

As mentioned previously, the highest age level considered in this book is twelve, an age reached by most children in the last year of elementary school (sixth grade). Children's sports, as conceived here, are not a prominent part of most elementary school programs. There are a few remote instances in which elementary schools support an interscholastic or varsity sports program, but for the most part this is quite rare. On the other hand, the major emphasis is placed on a well-balanced physical education program where all children have an equal opportunity to participate. However, some elementary schools provide sports programs in the form of *intramural* activities. This is an outgrowth of physical education programs with teams organized so that one classroom may play against another. This usually occurs after school and is supervised by school officials.

The great preponderance of children's sports programs take place outside the school and are not ordinarily conducted under the supervision of the school. They are usually sponsored by recreation centers, business enterprises, and assorted boys' and girls' clubs.

Over the years such organizations as Little League baseball, Midget football, Pop Warner football, Itty Bitty basketball, Pee Wee golf, along with a vast host of others, have flourished and attracted children in fantastically large numbers, which some estimates place in excess of thirty million.

HISTORICAL BACKGROUND

Contrary to some general belief, sports experience for children is not of recent origin. In fact, educators and philosophers as far back as the early Greeks felt that sports-oriented activities might be a welcome adjunct to the total education of children. For instance, more than 2,300 years ago, Plato suggested that all early education should be a sort of play and develop around play situations.

In the seventeenth century, Locke, an English philosopher, felt that children should get plenty of exercise and learn to swim early in life. Rousseau, the notable French writer, held much the same opinion, believing that learning should develop from the enjoyable physical activities of childhood. These men, along with numerous others, influenced to some extent the path that children's sports has followed.

There have been periods in our history when any type of sports program was abandoned purely on the basis that body pleasure of any sort must be subjugated because this activity was associated with evil doing. The early American pioneers more or less typified this kind of puritanical thinking because there was little or no emphasis on sports for the pioneer child.

Eventually, however, attitudes changed and interest in children's sports began to emerge. Instrumental in the movement was the establishment of the first public playground, Boston Sand Gardens, in Boston in 1885. This idea soon spread nationwide with children from one playground competing in various sports activities with those from other playgrounds.

It was not long before enterprising merchants saw possibilities for advertising by sponsoring various teams, thus capitalizing by organizing the traditional neighborhood games of children. It certainly made any child proud to be wearing a team shirt with "Hoopengartner's grocery" or "Norton's drugstore" emblazoned on the back.

In more modern times a much different outlook has characterized the area of children's sports, and much of this involves the physical fitness of children. In fact, over a period of several years there have been varying degrees of interest in the physical fitness of children and youth. In the early 1950s, the publication of the results of six physical fitness evaluations called the Kraus-Weber tests (named after their authors) stimulated a great deal of concern about physical fitness of

American children. These tests had been administered to large numbers of European children, and comparisons made with the results of the tests administered to a sample of children in Westchester County, New York, showed that the American children scored appreciably lower. The fact that this geographical area at the time was considered to be one of the country's highest socioeconomic levels made the comparison all the more "appalling."

The validity and reliability of these tests, as well as the conditions under which they were administered, tended to arouse criticism among some of the skeptics of that time. Nonetheless, the results did serve the purpose of alerting American educators and laypeople alike to the alleged declining physical status of the nation's children.

As a result, then President Dwight D. Eisenhower appointed Shane McCarthy, a Washington, DC, lawyer, to head a committee on Fitness of American Children and Youth. Among others, this committee consisted of assorted professional boxers and a famous racehorse trainer. Although the intentions of these individuals were not necessarily questioned, at the same time their knowledge and understanding of childhood fitness was of some concern. Since that time the various chairpersons of The President's Council on Physical Fitness and Sports have been appointed mainly because of their public exposure rather than their knowledge of fitness of children.

Another event stimulated by the results of the Kraus-Weber tests was the President's Conference on Fitness of American Youth held in Annapolis, Maryland, June 18 and 19, 1956. This was the first peacetime fitness conference ever held under White House auspices, and it helped to arouse public interest in childhood fitness.

A short time later, in September 1956, I was one of 100 so-called experts who convened in Washington, DC, to study the problem of fitness for children. This conference had a great deal of impact on the improvement of existing elementary school physical education programs as well as out-of-school sports programs.

Over the years after this thrust, childhood fitness through sports has experienced various degrees of success, interest has continued, and as a result at the present time children's sports are enjoying almost unprecedented enthusiasm.

IMPORTANT ASPECTS OF CHILDREN'S SPORTS

Adults should be concerned with a number of factors when they become involved in children's sports: competition, injury, supervision, interest, and positive and negative repercussions.

Competition

Sports competition for children has been debated for decades. In fact, over forty years ago I was the chairman of a national committee on competition for children. After studying the matter with some degree of thoroughness, the "experts" on our committee decided that the success or failure of such competition was dependent upon the type of supervision provided for overseeing such programs. (Supervision of children's sports is discussed later in this chapter.)

There has always been a concern for the emotional stress that competition can have on a child. And, of course, such emotional stress can impact on a child's physical well-being.

In a study conducted with 200 fifth and sixth grade children, one of the questions I asked was, "What is the one thing that *worries* you most in school?" As might be expected there were a variety of responses. However, the one general characteristic that tended to emerge was the emphasis placed on competition in so many school situations. Although students did not state this specifically, the nature of their responses were clearly along these lines.

Most of the literature on competition for children has focused on sports activities; however, many situations exist in some classrooms that can cause competitive stress. An example is the antiquated "spelling bee," which still exists in some schools; in fact, it continues to be recognized in an annual national competition. Perhaps the first few children "spelled down" are likely the ones who need the most spelling practice. With this exercise, they receive the least help, and it is embarrassing to fail in front of others in any school task.

The reconciliation of children's competitive needs and cooperative needs is not an easy matter. In a sense we are confronted with an ambivalent condition which, if not carefully handled, could place children in a state of conflict, thus causing them to suffer distress.

This was recognized by Horney over half a century ago when she indicated that we must not only be assertive but aggressive, able to push others out of the way.[1] On the other hand, we are deeply imbued with ideals which declare that it is selfish to want anything for ourselves, that we should be humble, turn the other cheek, be yielding. Thus society not only rewards one kind of behavior (cooperation) but also its direct opposite (competition). Perhaps our cultural demands sanction these rewards without provision for clear-cut standards of value with regard to specific conditions under which these forms of behavior might well be practiced. Thus, the child is placed in somewhat of a quandary as to when it is best to compete and when to cooperate.

It has been found that competition does not necessarily lead to peak performance and may in fact interfere with achievement. In this connection, Kohn reported on a survey on the effects of competition in sports, business, and classroom achievement, and found that sixty-five studies showed that cooperation promoted higher achievement than competition, eight showed the reverse, and thirty-six showed no statistically significant differences.[2] It was concluded that the trouble with competition is that it makes one person's success depend upon another's failure, and as a result when success depends on sharing resources, competition can get in the way.

In studying about competitive stress, Scanlan and Passer describe this condition as occurring when children feel (perceive) that they will not be able to perform adequately to the performance demands of competition.[3] When they feel this way, they experience considerable threat to self-esteem, which results in stress. Scanlan and Passer further describe competitive stress as the negative emotion or anxiety that children experience when they perceive the competition to be personally threatening. Indeed, this is a condition that should not be allowed in any environment—in school or out of school.

Studying the problem objectively, Scanlan uses a sports environment to identify predictors of competitive stress.[4] She investigated the influence and stability of individual differences and situational factors on the competitive stress experienced by seventy-six nine- to fourteen-year-old wrestlers. The subjects represented sixteen teams from one state and reflected a wide range of wrestling ability and experience. Stress was assessed by the children's form of the Competitive State Anxiety Inventory and was measured immediately before and after each of two consecutive tournament matches.

The children's dispositions, characteristic precompetition cognitions, perceptions of significant adult influences, psychological states,

self-perceptions, and competitive outcomes were examined as predictors of pre- and postmatch anxiety in separate multiple regression
analyses for each tournament round. The most influential and stable
predictors of prematch stress for both matches were competitive stress
anxiety and personal performance expectancies, and win-loss and fun
experienced during the match predicted postmatch stress for both
rounds.

Prematch worries about failure and perceived parental pressure to
participate were predictive to round one prematch stress. Round one
postmatch stress levels predicted stress after round two, suggesting
some consistency in the children's stress responses. Sixty-one and 35
percent prematch and 41 and 32 percent of postmatch state anxiety
variances was explained for rounds one and two, respectively.

In generalizing on the basis of the available evidence with regard
to the subject of competition, it seems justifiable to formulate the following concepts.

1. Very young children, in general, are not very competitive but
   become more so as they grow older.
2. There is a wide variety in competition among children; that is,
   some are violently competitive, others are mildly competitive,
   and still others are not competitive at all.
3. In general, boys are more competitive than girls.
4. Competition should be adjusted so that there is not a preponder-
   ant number of winners over losers.
5. Competition and rivalry can sometimes produce results in effort
   and speed of accomplishment.

Adults involved in children's sports might well be guided by these
concepts. Whether a person is a proponent or critic of competitive
sports for children, it has now become evident that competition may
be "here to stay." Thus, controlling it might be our greatest concern.
This might perhaps be done by concentrating our efforts in the direction of educating both adults and children regarding the positive and
negative effects of competition.

Injury

The possibility of injury is of most concern to parents whose children participate in sports. It should be kept in mind that contrary to

popular opinion, accidents resulting in injury do not "just happen." On the other hand, many such accidents are caused. Although injuries do occur, many of them could be avoided by taking proper precautions. Thus, appropriate care should be taken to assure the well-being of the child participant.

Certain conditions are traditionally associated with sports. "Tennis elbow" is a case in point. This is an inflammation of the rounded portion of the bone at the elbow joint. The condition's name is a misnomer, because the majority of cases are a result of activities other than swinging a tennis racquet.

The same could probably be said of what has become commonly known as "Little League elbow." The technical name for this condition is *osteochondritis capitulum* which, like "tennis elbow," is an inflammation of a bone and its cartilage at the elbow joint. It is caused generally by a hard and prolonged act of throwing using the overarm throwing pattern. A child does not have to be a Little Leaguer to develop this condition. Simply playing catch and throwing hard to a partner for prolonged periods could also cause this.

In this particular regard it is interesting to note that some believe that childhood baseball pitchers should refrain from trying to throw curve balls. They feel that such a practice will cause children to injure their arms. For instance, one Major League pitcher, Tommy John, who won 288 games, is reputed to have recommended that players should wait until they are at least fourteen years of age before they throw curve balls, and then only under the guidance of an experienced coach.[5]

One of the most feared injuries in sports, or any activity for that matter, is an eye injury. In this regard Orland did an interesting study to determine the severity and frequency of soccer-related eye injuries.[6] The medical charts of thirteen soccer players who had sustained blunt trauma to the eye were reviewed. The patients (five girls, eight boys) ranged from eight to fifteen years old. The most common injury was *hyphema* (a hemorrhage in the eyeball). Others included *retinal edema* (excessive accumulation of fluid in the innermost layer of the eye), *secondary glaucoma* (increased pressure within the eyeball), *chorioretinal rupture* (an inflammatory condition in the back of the eye), and *angle recession*. Six injuries were caused by the soccer ball, three by a kick, and one by a head butt. In three cases the cause was unknown. As a result of the study, the author made the following recommendations: (1) education of coaching staff, parents, and officials; (2) protective eyewear; (3) proper conditioning; (4) strictly enforced rules; and (5) an emphasis on having fun to help reduce the number and severity of soccer-related eye injuries.

One very interesting concern was generated by spectators of the 1992 Olympic Games in Barcelona. They feared that the constant physical pounding associated with gymnastics could hurt female participants and impair their development. (Many children start taking gymnastics as early as age five, and sometimes younger.)

For more than forty years some critics have been concerned with possible injuries that children might sustain in contact sports, especially football. This concern has centered around the notion that too much pressure would be applied to the epiphyses, particularly in such activities as football.

In the long bones there is first a center of ossification for the bone called the *diaphysis* and one or more centers for each extremity called the *epiphysis*. Ossification proceeds from the diaphysis toward the epiphysis, and from the epiphysis toward the diaphysis. As each new portion is ossified, thin layers of cartilage continue to develop between the diaphysis and epiphysis; during this period of growth, these outstrip ossification. When this ceases, the growth of the bone stops. Injury can occur as a result of trauma, which could be due to a "blow" incurred in a contact sport.

Incidentally, a quarterback who played for several years in the National Football League told me that he had to "fight off" his own son's participation in football until the boy was almost fourteen years of age. He said he was forced to relent because of his child's loss of status among his peers.

If we are to be successful in our efforts to avoid injuries to child sports participants, more emphasis needs to be exerted in the direction of preventive measures. Such measures can be taken by those who have the direct responsibility of working with children in sports activities.

Supervision

In the present context, the term *supervision* is essentially concerned with those persons who coach or manage children's sports teams. I am frequently asked by parents about the advisability of their children's participation in sports. My immediate response is to find out the qualifications and objectives of those persons who will assume the responsibility for coaching.

In the past, this was a much more serious matter because some coaches had little experience—especially in how to deal with growing children in competitive situations. At the present time, however, this situation has been alleviated somewhat, mainly because of such organizations as the National Youth Sports Coaches Association (NYSCA). This is a nonprofit association that has proven to be a frontrunner in the development of a national training system for volunteer sports youth coaches.

One of my former students, Fred Engh, is the association's President/CEO. He has indicated to me that some 450,000 coaches have undertaken the NYSCA's three-year, three-level program to qualify for membership and certification. This certification program focuses on helping volunteer coaches understand the psychological, physical, and emotional impact they have on children ages six to twelve. The criteria for NYSCA certification and membership are reviewed by the NYSCA National Executive Board, which is composed of representatives from the fields of education, recreation, and sports law.

One of the important aspects of the NYSCA has been the development of a Coaches' Code of Ethics, which provides rules and regulations of the NYSCA that coaches are required to observe.

One of the problems with children's sports has been the attitude of some parents who seem to exhibit "parental pride in the parent" rather than "parental pride in the child." Aware of this, the NYSCA has also developed a Parents' Code of Ethics, which parents of participants are required to sign.

Little League Baseball, Inc., also provides important information for its managers in the form of such printed materials as *The Other Side—A Manager's Guide to Working with Little Leaguers; Little League Rules and Practices; Care and Conditioning of the Pitching Arm;* and *Play It Safe.*[7]

I am sure that we would like to think that those who supervise children's sports, particularly coaches, have the best interest of children as their objective. In this regard some studies have attempted to determine the coach-child relationship. In one such study the UCLA Sports Psychology Laboratory tried to determine attitudes of 2,000 Southern California boys and girls who participate in sports and found that the factor that contributed most to their enjoyment was "positive coach support."[8]

My own surveys of children's sports participants on this subject yielded some interesting results. On a scale with 4.0 being the highest, boys rated their coaches at 3.4 and girls gave them a 3.3 rating.

Boys gave the following answers to the question, "What do you like *best* about your coach?" The coach:

- is nice. (34 percent)
- is fair. (26 percent)
- teaches us good things. (26 percent)
- is funny. (7 percent)
- says it is all right if we lose. (7 percent)

Girls gave the following answers to the question. The coach:

- is nice. (42 percent)
- is funny. (28 percent)
- is fair. (14 percent)
- helps us play better. (10 percent)
- is young. (6 percent)

Boys gave the following answers to the question, "What do you like *least* about your coach?" The coach:

- gets mad and yells at us. (64 percent)
- works us too hard. (22 percent)
- doesn't let me play enough. (8 percent)
- is not a good teacher. (3 percent)
- doesn't praise us enough. (3 percent)

Girls answered the question as follows. The coach:

- gets mad and yells at us. (57 percent)
- doesn't teach us much. (19 percent)
- works us too hard. (14 percent)
- doesn't praise us enough. (5 percent)
- seems unhappy. (5 percent)

In attempting to verbalize all of these data, one could come up with all sorts of possibilities of how children characterize their coach. Here is one such possibility: *The coach is usually a nice person with a sense of humor who is generally fair but at the same time is likely to get mad and yell at the players.*

There is no question about it, the quality level of supervision is an important factor in children's sports. In the final analysis, the success or failure of any program will ultimately depend upon its contribution to the total development of the child.

Interest

For most children—boys and girls alike—sports rank high on their lists of interests. Traditionally, boys have been more interested in team sports, and girls find more interest in individual sports. In recent years, however, studies have shown an increasing interest among girls in team sports.

Periodically, over several years I have used my own Humphrey Children's Sports Inventory to conduct studies in this age range. My most recent survey was completed in the fall of 2001. These surveys have identified not only the sports in which children enjoy *participating,* but those which they are interested in *observing* as well. Although there are slight variations in interest among the age ranges (six to twelve), by and large the overall interests are essentially the same. Thus, the results reported here are for the entire age range.

Five Most Popular Team Sports Among Boys

1. Basketball
2. Football
3. Baseball
4. Soccer
5. Volleyball

Five Most Popular Team Sports Among Girls

1. Basketball
2. Softball
3. Volleyball
4. Soccer
5. Football

It is not surprising that basketball is the most popular team sport among both boys and girls, since it is truly an American game, having been invented by Dr. James Naismith of Springfield, Massachusetts, in 1891. What may be surprising to some readers is the interest of girls in football. This interest is concerned not only with girls as spectators but as participants as well. In fact, more and more girls are participating (with boys) in *touch* football, but not necessarily in the game of *tackle* football. At a higher age level there are exceptional instances where girls have "tried out" for the high school football team. A case in point is that of the high school female place kicker who doubled as homecoming queen at halftime.

The interest in soccer as a popular team sport among both boys and girls has risen appreciably in recent years. This can be attributed in part to the excellent showing of the U.S. team at the 2002 World Cup.

Five Most Popular Individual Sports Among Boys

1. Track and field
2. Swimming
3. Gymnastics
4. Golf
5. Fencing

Five Most Popular Individuals Sports Among Girls

1. Gymnastics
2. Swimming
3. Track and field
4. Golf
5. Fencing

The high interest in gymnastics and swimming among girls can perhaps be attributed to the fact that these are activities in which girls have traditionally excelled. Also, in recent years these sports have received a great deal of media attention.

It is easy to understand why track and field ranks so high, particularly with boys, because the basic skills of running and jumping are activities in which most boys like to engage.

One of the things that has changed our thinking about track events for children is *distance running*. A few years ago distance running for children was held in great disrepute, just as marathon running was for women. However, the past few years have seen a great change in attitude about distance running for children. The major reason for this appears to focus around the belief by some that health practices begun in early childhood are related to adult health and fitness. What we are essentially concerned with here is the *aerobic* fitness provided by distance running. Charles O. Dotson, my distinguished associate and co-editor of the research annual *Exercise Physiology: Current Selected Research,* asserts that evidence shows certain health and fitness characteristics track from childhood to adulthood.[9] Aerobic fitness is one of these characteristics. For example, a child who has above-average aerobic fitness can be expected to track to middle age at above-average aerobic fitness, and a child with below-average aerobic fitness can be expected to track to middle age at below-average aerobic fitness.

It is believed that a person needs to have forty-two milliliters of oxygen per kilogram of body weight per minute (42 ml/kg per min) to provide resistance against cardiovascular disease. In order to track to a level that is above forty-two ml, it is recommended that a person participate in aerobic activity fitness three times per week for twenty to thirty minute periods.

Children should be provided with knowledge and motivation to develop habitual physical activity over and above that provided in regular school physical education classes. Thus, children should have the opportunity to participate in out-of-school aerobic activities. Children who participate with parents who are fit are more likely to be fit than children who do not do so. Moreover, the more that community programs provide opportunities for physical activity in the form of aerobics for children, the more such children are likely to be aerobically fit.

The test batteries developed for fitness of children now include a measure of aerobic fitness, usually in the form of a distance run/walk item. Among the organizations that provide for tests of fitness for children are the American Alliance for Health, Physical Education, Recreation, and Dance (Physical Best), and the Institute for Aerobic Research (Fitnessgram). Although the majority of fitness assessment batteries now include grades kindergarten through four (K-4), there is not a great deal of scientific evidence to substantiate the practicality, reliability, or validity of the various test items for children at these early age levels. In this general regard, Rikli, Petray, and Baumgartner conducted a study of the reliability of distance running tests for children in grades K-4.[10] The purpose of this study was to determine test-retest reliability for the one-mile, three-quarter-mile, and half-mile distance run/walk tests for children in grades K-4. Fifty-one intact physical education classes were randomly assigned to one of the three distance run conditions. A total of 1,229 (621 boys, 608 girls) completed the test-retests in the fall (October), with 1,050 of these students (543 boys, 507 girls) repeating the tests the following spring (May).

The researchers concluded that results of this study indicate that the distance run can be utilized as a reliable assessment tool for students in grades K-4 when appropriate age/distance adjustments are made. The one-mile run/walk has acceptable norm-referenced reliability for students in grades 3 and 4, with the half-mile the longest acceptable distance for students in grades K and 1. For students in grade 2, the half- and three-quarter-mile tests tend to be the most reliable with respect to overall estimates across both males and females in the fall. By the end of the school year (May), the three-quarter and one-mile tests tend to have the best overall reliabilities for second graders. It might be argued that the three-quarter-mile run/walk should be the recommended distance for grade 2 students, both with respect to test reliability and as a logical transition between the half-mile distance in grades K and 1 and the one-mile test in grades 3 and 4.

Results of the study also indicate that test scores for most age/gender groups, with some exceptions for ages five and six on the one-mile test, are acceptably reliable in their classifications of students with respect to meeting the standards for the Physical Best and Fitnessgram national test batteries.

Another individual sport that has emerged as extremely popular for children is golf. Of course, the main reason for this is the emergence of Tiger Woods as the world's premier golfer. When children see him on television at the age of three learning the game of golf, many of them are also inspired to do so. Thus, golf programs for children have increased at an unprecedented rate.

One of the greatest surprises in my most recent surveys was the increase in popularity of the sport of fencing. Many parents are interested in this sport for their children because they feel that children are not at so great a risk for injury. A testimony of this sport's popularity is shown in the fact that the number of children belonging to the United States Fencing Association has doubled in the past few years.

Positive and Negative Repercussions

I have discussed children's participation in sports with both proponents and critics, and both attempt to make a compelling case for their particular philosophy. Most of the support is based only on opinion gained from experience because there is very little hard objective evidence to support one position over another.

Even some of the strongest supporters of children's sports are likely to raise certain precautions about such participation. For example, a children's organization proclaims that sports help children develop physical skills, get exercise, make friends, learn to play fair, and improve self-esteem. At the same time this organization suggests that the highly stressful competitive "win at all cost" attitude affects the world of children's sports, creating an unhealthy environment.

A private physician believes that children active in sports programs will improve their cardiovascular and musculoskeletal systems, state of mind, self-discipline, and recognition of the importance of a healthy body. However, he emphasizes that such participation can predispose children to injuries, the effect of which can last a lifetime.

The worst-case scenario with regard to children's sports is seen in such recent headlines as "Coach Breaks Child's Arm" and "Fan Assaults Son's Coach with Knife." Indeed, there is an "ugly" side to children's sports. Some persons lay a part of the blame on parents who will stop at nothing to push their children unmercifully to be star athletes and will cheat, bend the rules, and even risk the safety of children. Although such cases may be few in number, even that they exist at all is a sad commentary on an activity that has potential benefits for children.

Finally, it is the responsibility of those adults who are involved in children's sports to provide an environment that will always be in the best interest of the child. In this regard, all of us might well consider the words of the old popular song, "accentuate the positive, eliminate the negative," as a basic guideline in conducting children's sports programs.

Chapter 5

Objectives of Children's Sports

The component elements of total development can satisfactorily emerge as valid sports objectives for children. These elements have been expressed in terms of physical, social, emotional, and intellectual development constituting the total personality. As such, they can logically become the physical, social, emotional, and intellectual objectives of sports for children.

The term *objective* appears to have been adopted by education from the military. The military uses it to identify areas to be assaulted and/or captured in some way. The *Dictionary of Education* defines the term as "aim, end in view, or purpose of a course of action or a belief; that which is anticipated as desirable in the early phases of an activity and serves to select, regulate, and direct later aspects of the act so that the total process is designed and integrated."[1] Various other terms are used to convey the same meaning. Some of these include *goal* and *purpose*. Regardless of the particular terms used, we might well consider it with regard to a very simple meaning; that is, what should we be trying to accomplish through the sports medium where total development of children is concerned?

PHYSICAL OBJECTIVES

A good sports program for children can be considered as a stimulant to physical growth. Moreover, the general consensus indicates that participation in a well-balanced sports program could be a good way of maintaining optimum health.

It should be kept in mind that some children have great physical advantages simply because of the particular body build they may happen to have, and others may be at a relatively great disadvantage because of a very heavyset or slight body build. Consequently, our objective should not be to make *every* child a great athlete. Rather, the physical objectives must be to help *each* child who participates to develop his or her individual potentialities for controlled and effective body movement as fully as possible.

Two major objectives emerge out of the physical aspect of personality: maintaining a suitable level of physical fitness and development of skill and ability.

Maintaining a Suitable Level of Physical Fitness

Physical fitness presupposes adequate nutrition and an adequate amount of rest and sleep, but, beyond these things, activity involving all the big muscles of the body is also essential. Just how high a level of physical fitness should be maintained from one stage of life to another is difficult to answer, because we must raise the question, "Fitness for what?"

Physical fitness has been perceived in different ways by different people. However, when all of these descriptions are put together, it is likely that they will be characterized more by their similarities than by their differences. For purposes here, let us think of physical fitness as the level of ability of the human organism to perform certain physical tasks, or, put another way, the fitness to perform various specified tasks requiring muscular effort.

A reasonable question to raise at this point is, "Why is a reasonably high level of physical fitness desirable in modern times when so many effort-saving devices are available that, for many people, strenuous activity is really not necessary anymore?" One possible answer to this is because all of us stand at the end of a long line of ancestors, all of whom at least lived long enough to have children. They were fit and vigorous and strong enough to survive in the face of savage beasts and savage men, in addition to hard work. Only the fit survived. Not very far back in your own family tree you would find people who had to be rugged and extremely active in order to live. Vigorous action and physical ruggedness are our biological heritage. Possibly, because of the kind of background that we have, our bodies simply function better when we are active.

Many child development specialists agree that vigorous play in childhood is essential for the satisfactory growth of the various organs and systems of the body. It has been said that play is the business of childhood. To conduct this business successfully and happily, children should be physically fit. Good nutrition, rest, and properly conducted sports programs have the potential to do much to develop and maintain the physical fitness of children.

Development of Skill and Ability

The second major physical objective of children's sports has to do with disciplined bodily movement. Physically educated children, commensurate with their capacities and within their own limitations, are adept in a variety of sports activities. Children enjoy those activities in which they are reasonably proficient. Thus, we are dealing with an important principle related to our children's sports objectives; that is, if children are to enjoy participating in sports activities, they need to be reasonably competent in the skills involved in these activities. Consequently, there must be objectives both in terms of the number of skills to which children at the different age levels are introduced and the level of competence to be achieved at that age level so that they may associate a pleasurable experience with participation.

We must reckon with another matter that is closely related to competence in a wide variety of skills. Some organizations have stressed the very strenuous team sports in their programs and others have placed emphasis on what have been called "lifetime sports" that may be used in later life. A sensible point of view on this subject is that we should develop competence in a variety of skills for use "now *and* in the future." Stated more specifically, as an objective of children's sports it could be said that all children should be prepared by their sports experience to participate in suitable and satisfying activities for use now and in the future. Those individuals who would place undue emphasis on strenuous violent activities at the expense of lifetime activities for use in the future should pay special attention to the word *suitable* in the previous sentence. What is suitable during one period of life is not necessarily suitable during another. The intensely competitive, vigorous, and—in some cases—violent sports are considered by some to be unsuitable, especially for young children.

In summary, the physical objective of children's sports should imply organic development commensurate with vigor, vitality, strength, balance, flexibility, and neuromuscular coordination, together with the development of skill and ability in a variety of activities for use now and in the future.

SOCIAL OBJECTIVES

The sports "laboratory" (areas where activities take place) should present near ideal surroundings and environment for the social development of children. Why are people who are in the field of children's sports convinced that this area provides some of the very best means of teaching vital social skills? By their very nature, sports activities are essentially socially oriented. If any type of sports experience is to be successful and satisfying, the children involved must possess or acquire considerable skill in dealing with one another. They must learn to work together for the interest of the group; accept and respect the rules of the games that they play; learn that sometimes it is necessary to place the welfare of the group ahead of their own personal desires; respect the rights of others; think and plan with the group and for the group; and learn to win and lose gracefully.

In looking over this list of social skills that is important in children's sports, it should be discerned that such social skills are necessary for happy and successful living everywhere. A qualified children's sports coach or manager should find numerous opportunities to develop skills of interpersonal relationships that far exceed the basic essentials for successful play. Indeed, successful children's sports coaches and managers should consider the development of increased social awareness and social skills as important objectives of their programs, and they should make specific plans to reach these objectives. They should recognize that children's sports can have a profoundly humanizing effect upon children; participants quickly learn to evaluate their team members on the basis of what they can do and what kind of person they are rather than on the basis of their looks, race, religion, color, or economic status.

A brief summary of the social objectives of children's sports might imply satisfactory experiences in meeting and getting along with others, developing proper attitudes toward one's peers, and developing a sense of social values.

EMOTIONAL OBJECTIVES

Some sports experiences can be emotional situations. For the child, there is the excitement that may be felt before certain kinds of sports activities are initiated. When play is in progress, there is the thrill of making skillful moves and the possible disappointments or frustrations when he or she does not do well. Finally, the after-play emotions are determined to some extent by how well the child performed in relation to how well he or she expects to perform, but in almost all instances these emotions include pleasure caused by the good feeling that the time was well spent.

With regard to the foregoing comments, the results of my surveys are of interest. Forty percent of the boys and 37 percent of the girls reported that they were "very nervous" before a game. Moreover, 31 percent of the boys and 17 percent of the girls felt pressure to win from their parents and/or coaches.

Boys gave the following answers to the question, "How do you feel when you win?"

- Good (42 percent)
- Happy (38 percent)
- Great (18 percent)
- Like I did my best (2 percent)

Girls essentially displayed the same pleasant emotions with the following answers.

- Happy (41 percent)
- Good (40 percent)
- Great (16 percent)
- OK (3 percent)

Boys gave the following anwers to the question, "How do you feel when you lose?"

- Bad (32 percent)
- Sad (16 percent)
- OK (16 percent)
- No feelings (9 percent)

- Fine (7 percent)
- Unhappy (7 percent)
- Good (6 percent)
- Like I want to kill myself (5 percent)
- Disgusted (2 percent)

Girls expressed some of the same unpleasant emotions as the boys, but for the most part they did not find losing as distressful as witnessed by the largest percentage feeling "OK" about it.

- OK (33 percent)
- Bad (24 percent)
- Sad (16 percent)
- Mad (7 percent)
- Upset (5 percent)
- Great (3 percent)
- Good (2 percent)
- Unhappy (2 percent)
- No feelings (2 percent)
- Disappointed (2 percent)
- Stupid (1 percent)
- Embarrassed (1 percent)
- Dumb (1 percent)
- Fine (1 percent)

There are two very important things that might be accomplished with the emotional aspect of personality. These may be classified as (1) to provide for fun and emotional release, and (2) to develop an increased capacity to control emotions, thus contributing to the development of emotional maturity.

Fun and Emotional Release

Certainly one of the most important objectives of children's sports should be fun. Moreover, children's sports should provide opportunities for children to enjoy uninhibited and vigorous movement. Because of their very nature, children require vigorous activity for proper growth and development. *They should not sit and watch television for prolonged periods without such activity!* (Many of them do, however.) Children's sports should be primarily a learning experience for them, but their value as a means of easing emotional tensions in the form of genuine fun certainly should not be underestimated. My studies show that 53 percent of the girls and 48 percent of the boys participate in sports because of the fun they derive from them.

Emotional Control

The difference between a so-called normal individual and an incorrigible one is that the former has the ability to control his or her emotional impulses to a greater extent than the latter. Perhaps all of us at one time or another have experienced the same kind of emotions that have led the abnormal individual to commit violence, but we have been able to hold our powerful and violent emotions in check. This may be an extreme example, but it should suggest something of the importance of emotional control.

Children's sports should help them increase their capacity to handle and control their emotions. Thoughtful coaches or managers are aware of opportunities offered in play situations for children to learn to deal with their emotional arousals in socially acceptable ways. They help guide children in such a way that they will learn to take pride in their ability to restrain themselves when necessary in order to abide by the rules of fair play and to behave as reasonable and decent human beings. Coaches or managers have real emotionally charged situations with which to work in order to teach children to deal with their strong emotions.

Another aspect of controlling the emotions is becoming able to function effectively and intelligently in an emotionally charged situation. Sometimes success in children's sports experiences may hinge upon this ability, as does success in many other life situations. Extremes of emotional upset must be avoided if children are able to think and act effectively. In sports situations, children should learn that if they immediately put their minds to work on other things, such as group cooperation, they can control their emotions.

In summary, sympathetic guidance should be provided in meeting anxieties, joys, and sorrows, and help should be given in developing aspirations, affections, and security.

INTELLECTUAL OBJECTIVES

Intellectual development has been subjected to a great deal of criticism by some individuals. However, sports are not "all brawn and no brain" activities. Close scrutiny of the possibilities of intellectual development through children's sports reveals, however, that a very desirable contribution can be made through this medium.

In a well-planned sports experience, there are numerous opportunities to exercise judgment and resort to reflective thinking in the solution of various kinds of problems. In addition, in a well-balanced program, children must acquire a knowledge of certain rules and regulations in the games that they play. It is also essential for effective participation that children gain an understanding of the various fundamentals and strategy involved in the performance of certain kinds of sports activities.

In summary, the intellectual objectives of children's sports imply the development of specific knowledge pertaining to rules, regulations, and strategies involved in a variety of worthwhile experiences. In addition, the objectives should be concerned with the value of children's sports as a learning medium in the development of certain intellectual concepts and understandings.

Chapter 6

Physical Development

Physical development is concerned with the child's physical ability to function at an increasingly higher level. For example, a stage of development in the infant is from creeping to crawling. This is later followed by walking, when the child moves to an upright position and begins to move over the surface area by putting one foot in front of the other.

PHYSICAL NEEDS

If any physical values are to accrue from children's sports, it becomes imperative that such sports be planned on the basis of the physical needs of children. These needs are reflected in physical development.

The following lists of physical characteristics have been developed through a documentary analysis of more than a score of sources that have appeared in the literature on child development over the years. It should be understood that these characteristics are suggestive of the behavior patterns of so-called normal children. This implies that if children do not conform to these characteristics, it should not be interpreted to mean that they are seriously deviating from the normal. In other words, it should be recognized that individuals progress at their own rate and there can be overlapping characteristics for each of the age levels. In examining these lists, adults should attempt to determine the extent to which a given sport *contributes* or *detracts* from them.

Five-Year-Old Children

1. Boys' height, 42 to 46 inches; weight, 38 to 49 pounds; girls' height, 42 to 46 inches; weight, 36 to 48 pounds
2. May grow two or three inches and gain three to six pounds throughout the year

3. Girls about a year ahead of boys in physiological development
4. Beginning to have better control of body
5. Better development of the large muscles than the small muscles that control the fingers and hands
6. Usually determined whether they will be right- or left-handed
7. Incomplete eye-hand coordination
8. May have farsighted vision
9. Vigorous and noisy, but activity appears to have definite direction
10. Tire easily and need plenty of rest

Six-Year-Old Children

1. Boys' height, 44 to 48 inches; weight, 41 to 54 pounds; girls' height, 43 to 48 inches; weight, 40 to 53 pounds
2. Gradual growth in height and weight
3. Good supply of energy
4. Marked activity urges; children absorbed in running, jumping, chasing, and dodging games
5. Muscular control with large objects becoming more effective
6. Noticeable change in eye-hand behavior
7. Legs lengthening rapidly
8. Big muscles crave activity

Seven-Year-Old Children

1. Boys' height, 46 to 51 inches; weight, 45 to 60 pounds; girls' height, 46 to 50 inches; weight, 44 to 59 pounds
2. Big muscle activity interest and value high
3. More improvement in eye-hand coordination
4. May grow two or three inches and gain three to five pounds throughout the year.
5. Tire easily and show fatigue in the afternoon
6. Have slow reaction time
7. Heart and lungs are small in proportion to body size
8. General health may be precarious; susceptibility to disease high and resistance low
9. Endurance relatively low
10. Coordination improving with throwing; catching becoming more accurate

11. Whole-body movements under better control
12. Small accessory muscles developing
13. Display amazing amounts of vitality

Eight-Year-Old Children

1. Boys' height, 48 to 53 inches; weight, 49 to 70 pounds; girls' height, 48 to 52 inches; weight 47 to 66 pounds
2. Interested in games requiring coordination of small muscles
3. Arms lengthening and hands growing larger
4. Eyes can accommodate more easily
5. Poor posture in some children
6. Frequent accidents at this age
7. Appreciate correct skill performance

Nine-Year-Old Children

1. Boys' height, 50 to 55 inches; weight, 55 to 74 pounds; girls' height, 50 to 54 inches; weight, 52 to 74 pounds
2. Increasing strength in arms, hands, and fingers
3. Endurance improving
4. Need and enjoy much activity; boys like to shout, wrestle, and tussle with one another
5. A few girls near puberty
6. Girls gaining growth maturity up to two years over boys
7. Girls enjoy group games but are usually less noisy and less full of spontaneous energy than boys
8. Likely to slouch and assume unusual postures
9. Eyes much better developed and able to accommodate to close work with less strain
10. May tend to overexercise
11. Sex differences appear in recreational activities
12. Interested in their own bodies and want to have questions answered

Ten-Year-Old Children

1. Boys' height, 52 to 57 inches; weight 59 to 82 pounds; girls' height, 52 to 57 inches; weight 57 to 83 pounds
2. Individuality well-defined, insights more mature

3. Stability in growth rate and stability of physiological processes
4. Physically active and like to rush around and be busy
5. Before onset of puberty there is usually a resting period or plateau, during which boys or girls do not appear to gain in either height or weight
6. Interested in the development of more skills
7. Reaction time improving
8. Muscular strength slower to develop than body growth
9. Refining and elaborating skill in the use of small muscles

Eleven-Year-Old Children

1. Boys' height, 53 to 58 inches; weight, 64 to 91 pounds; girls' height, 53 to 59 inches; weight, 64 to 95 pounds
2. Marked changes in muscle system causing awkwardness and habits sometimes distressing to the child
3. Show fatigue more easily
4. Rapid growth in some girls and a few boys; evidence of the approach of adolescence
5. On average, girls taller and heavier than boys
6. Uneven growth of different parts of the body
7. Laziness in lateral-type children and fatigue and irritability in linear-type children due to rapid growth
8. Willing to work hard at acquiring physical skills, and emphasis on excellence of performance of physical feats
9. Boys more active and rough in games than girls
10. Eye-hand coordination well developed
11. Body growth more rapid than heart growth; lungs not fully developed
12. Boys develop greater power in shoulder girdle muscles

Twelve-Year-Old Children

1. Boys' height, 55 to 61 inches; weight, 70 to 101 pounds; girls' height, 56 to 62 inches; weight, 72 to 107 pounds
2. Becoming more skillful in the use of small muscles
3. May be relatively little body change
4. Ten hours of sleep considered average
5. Heart rate at rest between eighty and ninety

These heights and weights listed are what might be called a range within a range, and are computed means or averages within larger ranges. In other words, some children at a given age level could possibly weigh much more or less and be much taller or shorter than the ranges indicate. To illustrate how wide a range can be, one study of a large number of children showed that eleven-year-old girls ranged in weight from 46 to 180 pounds.

In those sports organizations in which a concentrated effort is made to conduct programs to meet the physical needs of all children, there is a strong likelihood that desirable contributions are being made to physical development. On the contrary, some sports programs as now operated cannot be justified as contributing to physical development of all children.

GUIDELINES FOR PHYSICAL DEVELOPMENT

It is important to set forth some guidelines for physical development if we are to meet with any degree of success in our attempts to provide for physical development of children through sports. The reason for this is to assure, at least to some extent, that our efforts in attaining optimum physical development through sports will be based upon a scientific approach. These guidelines might well take the form of valid concepts of physical development. This approach enables us to give serious consideration to what is known about how children grow and develop. Thus, we can select sports experiences that are compatible with the physical developmental process. The following list of concepts of physical development are accompanied by certain implications for children's sports.

1. *Physical development and change is continuous, orderly, progressive, and differentiated.* In the early years, sports programs, if considered at all, might well be characterized by large muscle activities. As the child develops, more difficult types of skills and activities can be introduced so that sports experiences progress in a way that is compatible with his or her development.

2. *Physical development is controlled by both heredity and environment.* The sports program should be planned in such a way as to contribute to the innate capacities of each child. Attempts should be made to establish an environment in which all children have an equal

opportunity for wholesome participation. Some organizations and leagues require that every child be allowed to participate at least some of the time. This means that no one will spend all of his or her time "warming the bench." In this regard the following study by Martens and colleagues is of interest.[1] They found that younger children often have problems playing baseball using adult rules because pitchers lack the ability to throw consistently and batters have trouble hitting erratically thrown balls. A modification of adult rules allowed the team coach to pitch to batters. More offensive and defensive activity occurred in the nontraditional games than in traditional and older-league games.

3. *Differences in physical development occur at each age level.* This implies that there should be a wide variety of activities to meet the needs of children at various developmental levels. Most of the children that I surveyed played three sports and sometimes more. As sports activities are geared to meet the needs of a particular group of children, attempts should also be made to provide for individual differences of children within the group. It is extremely important to classify children's sports teams for competition on the basis of physical fitness, skill level, and biological age—not on chronological age only. Also participants should be encouraged to participate in different sports and experience different positions within a given sports activity.

4. *Needs of a physical nature must be satisfied if a child is to function effectively.* Sports experiences should be planned to provide an adequate activity yield. (Physical activity yield will be discussed in detail later in the chapter.) Sports activities should be vigorous enough to meet the physical needs of children and, at the same time, motivating enough so that they will desire to perpetuate the sports experience at home and in their own neighborhood.

5. *Various parts of the body develop at different rates and at different ages.* Undue strain to the point of excessive fatigue should be avoided in sports activities. Coaches and parents should be aware of fatigue symptoms so that children are not likely to go beyond their physical capacity. Perhaps the use of large muscles should predominate sports activities, at least for children in the five- to eight-year-old age range.

6. *The individual's own growth pattern will vary from that of others both as to time and rate.* It is acceptable to compare a child's performance with his or her own previous achievements rather than that

of peers. The same standards of performance should not be expected from all children in any given activity due to individual differences. This is one of the important features of activities such as gymnastics, which allows children to compete against themselves as well as against natural forces.

7. *There are early maturers and late maturers.* This concept suggests the importance of proper grouping of children within given sports activities. The coach and parent should be aware as to when it is most profitable to classify children either homogeneously or heterogeneously for certain kinds of sports activities. The same thing applies here as in concept three.

8. *The level of physical maturation of the child often has a significant effect on learning.* Children should not be expected to achieve beyond their ability levels. A critical examination of their physical needs should be useful in applying this concept.

9. *Physical differences may have a marked effect on personality.* A variety of sports experiences should be provided in an effort to give children a chance to find some successful achievement within their own physical capacities. The coach should set the example for children to learn to be respectful of physical differences by helping them use their particular body type in the most advantageous way.

When sports programs for children are planned and implemented on the basis of what is known about how they grow and develop, greater contributions can be made to their physical development. Adherence to valid concepts of physical development is considered one of the best ways of accomplishing this goal.

EVALUATING CONTRIBUTIONS OF SPORTS TO PHYSICAL DEVELOPMENT

Some attempt should be made to assess the potential contribution made by those sports experiences that we provide for children. One of the first steps in this direction is to consider the physical objectives, or what we are trying to do for children physically. The broad physical objectives of children's sports suggested in the preceding chapter consisted of (1) maintaining a suitable level of physical fitness and (2) developing skill and ability.

In determining whether sports experiences are contributing to the child's physical fitness, consideration needs to be given to the identification of specific components constituting the broad aspect of physical fitness. As mentioned previously, there is not complete agreement with the identification of the components of physical fitness. However, the following information, provided by the President's Council of Physical Fitness and Sports, considers certain components to be basic.

1. *Muscular strength.* This refers to the contraction power of the muscles. The strength of muscles is usually measured by dynamometers or tensiometers, which record the amount of force particular muscle groups can apply in a single maximum effort. Our existence and effectiveness depend upon our muscles. All movements of the body or any of its parts are impossible without action of muscles attached to the skeleton. Muscles perform vital functions of the body as well. The heart is a muscle; death occurs when it ceases to contract. Breathing, digestion, and elimination are impossible without muscular contractions. These vital muscular functions are influenced by exercising the skeletal muscles; the heart beats faster, the blood circulates through the body at a greater rate, breathing comes deep and rapid, and perspiration breaks out on the surface of the skin.

2. *Muscular endurance.* Muscular endurance is the ability of the muscles to perform work. Two variations of muscular endurance are recognized: isometric, whereby a maximum static muscular contraction is held; isotonic, whereby the muscles continue to raise and lower a submaximal load, as in weight training or performing push-ups. In the isometric form, the muscles maintain a fixed length; in the isotonic form, they alternately shorten and lengthen. Muscular endurance must assume some muscle strength. However, there are distinctions between the two. Muscle groups of the same strength may possess different degrees of endurance.

3. *Circulatory-respiratory endurance.* Circulatory-respiratory endurance is characterized by moderate contractions of large muscle groups for relatively long periods of time during which maximal adjustment of the circulatory-respiratory system to the activity are necessary, as in distance running or swimming. Obviously, strong and enduring muscles are needed. However, by themselves, they are not enough; they do not guarantee well-developed circulatory and respiratory functions.

In addition to these, other components of physical fitness to be considered are listed next:

1. *Muscular power.* Ability to release maximum muscular force in the shortest time. Example—standing long jump.
2. *Agility.* Speed in changing direction, or body position. Example—dodging run.
3. *Speed.* Rapidity with which successive movements of the same kind are performed. Example—fifty-yard dash.
4. *Flexibility.* Range of movements in a joint or sequence of joints. Example—touch fingers to floor without bending knees.
5. *Balance.* Ability to maintain position, and equilibrium both in movement (dynamic balance) and while stationary (static balance). Example—walking on a line or balance beam (dynamic); standing on one foot (static).
6. *Coordination.* Working together of the muscles and organs of the human body in the performance of a specific task. Example—throwing or catching an object.

Having an understanding of these components of physical fitness should be extremely helpful to adults in their efforts to evaluate the extent to which certain sports experiences contribute to the maintenance of a suitable level of physical fitness. In fact, in planning sports experiences for children, certain questions may be raised in connection with the activities used to bring about these experiences.

1. Does the activity provide for contraction power of muscles (muscular strength)?
2. Are there opportunities in the activity for isometric and/or isotonic muscular activity (muscular endurance)?
3. Does the activity provide for moderate contraction of large muscles for specified periods of time (circulatory-respiratory endurance)?
4. Does the activity involve ability to release maximum muscular force in a short period of time (muscular power)?
5. Is there opportunity in the activity to utilize speed in changing direction (agility)?

6. Does the activity require rapidity with successive movements of the same kind (speed)?
7. Does the activity involve various degrees of bending at the joints (flexibility)?
8. Is the activity one that involves the ability to maintain position and equilibrium (balance)?
9. Is the activity concerned with the working together of the muscles and organs in specific task performance (coordination)?

Of course, it is not expected that all activities will involve all of the components of physical fitness. For example, although a certain sports activity may require various degrees of agility, it may not necessarily involve a great deal of muscular strength. However, it would be possible to select enough activities with sufficient balance of the components over a period of time so that they as a group could contribute to the total physical fitness of the child.

The adult should consider this approach not only in planning and practicing activities but also for purposes of value assessment after activities have been conducted. With this procedure, some judgment could be made with reference to how well the activity attained its purpose. Keep in mind that the extent to which a sports activity may contribute to any given component of physical fitness will be contingent upon a variety of factors: the ability level of a given group of children; the number of children on a team; the general nature of the activity; the difficulty in providing for individual differences; where the activity takes place; and, above all, the coach's input and behavior.

The second aspect of physical development through sports—development of skill and ability—could be evaluated in the same general manner. Each sports activity could be analyzed to determine the extent to which the following skills are necessary for success in the activity: running, leaping, jumping, hopping, sliding, starting, stopping, dodging, pivoting, landing, falling, throwing, catching, and kicking.

Again, it is not expected that all sports activities will involve all of these skills. However, it would be possible to select enough activities with sufficient balance of the various skills over a period of time so the activities as a group could contribute to the development of skill and ability.

PHYSICAL ACTIVITY YIELD

Another approach in determining the extent to which children's sports contribute to physical fitness is one that I have identified as *physical activity yield.* This is concerned with the amount of time that a majority of children are meaningfully active in a given sports experience. The term *majority* can have a range of from more than half to all of the children on a team. Generally, the majority of children is considered to be 80 percent of them. This would mean that there would be activity yield for a team if four out of five children were meaningfully active at one time. *Meaningfully active* is interpreted as children being involved in a sports activity that has a specific purpose and objective.

Reflecting back to my own personal experience as a child, I was a centerfielder on a Class F sandlot baseball team in a large metropolitan area in the Midwest. I had very little action in this position probably because most of the opposing batters could not hit the ball that far. Thus, I stood there practically motionless for most of the game. Later, as a high school basketball player, I experienced a great deal of physical activity yield because I seemed to be running up and down the floor "forever." Many years later these experiences may no doubt have been what caused me to characterize the game of baseball in the following manner: two people play catch (pitcher and catcher) while a third person (batter) tries to prevent it. Seven others (basemen and fielders) stand and watch, and still eight others (opposing team) sit and watch.

It should be interesting to note that although the game of baseball tends to provide a relatively small amount of physical activity yield as previously described, it nevertheless is a popular activity—our national pastime, no less.

The physical activity yield approach differs appreciably from the previously mentioned approach in that it is not as precise and definitive; that is, it provides only for a recognition of general physical activity engaged in by children and not for specific physical fitness components. Neither does it provide for consideration of skills used in the various activities.

In any case, the important factor to consider is that some attempt be made to arrive at an evaluation of the extent to which sports activities contribute to the physical development of children. This, of course, requires that each sports activity be carefully analyzed for its potential contribution to physical development, along with how the activity should be conducted, so that the most desirable and worthwhile results will be obtained.

Chapter 7

Social Development

Social development is comprehensive and has been described in a number of ways: (1) a pattern of change exhibited by the individual as a result of his or her interaction with such forces as people, social institutions, social customs, and social organizations; (2) the entire series of normal progressive changes from birth to death in social behavior, feelings, attitudes, values, etc.; (3) the state of any moment of an individual's social or socially significant reaction, evaluated in accordance with what is regarded as normal for that culture; (4) the growth of the culture of the group in the direction of the more complete satisfaction of the needs of its members.[1]

Sports enthusiasts have generously praised this experience as an outstanding medium for contributing to social development of children. This was shown in my recent analysis of more than fifty books that deal in some way with children's physical activity programs, including sports. The purpose of this analysis was to identify declarative statements that proclaimed positive contributions to the various forms of development—physical, social, emotional, and intellectual. Forty-five percent of the total number of statements indicated contributions to social development, followed by physical development with 29 percent, emotional development with 17 percent, and intellectual development with 9 percent.

Although this attests to the subjective pronouncements of the social values of children's physical activity programs and sports, at the same time it is interesting to note that little research has been conducted to build an objective foundation under this long-held theoretical postulation. In order to examine this more thoroughly, I made a documentary analysis of children's physical activity programs and sports research. It was reported in the *Research Quarterly for Exercise and Sports* over a twenty-year period (eighty issues). Seven percent of all the studies reported met the criteria that was established to determine if a study was concerned with children six to twelve years old. Sixty-seven percent of this number dealt with whole or part of the physical aspect. This compared with 12 percent with the emotional aspect, 11 percent with the intellectual aspect, and 10 percent with the social aspect. Moreover, in a very small percentage of the cases it was demonstrated that physical activity and sports programs made significant contributions to social development.

Most of the research that has been done in this general area has been devoted to the relationship between social and physical factors. The majority of these findings show that the most popular children are those who are most adept in the performance of physical skills required in sports. In this regard, it is interesting to note that some studies reveal that both sexes express a preference for good school marks over excelling in sports and being popular. It has also been reported that many children selected as outstanding academically or athletically were listed as popular more often than children not in these categories. When outstanding students, athletes, and student-athletes (outstanding academically and athletically) are compared in popularity, it is generally found that among boys, athletes were somewhat more popular, and among girls, student-athletes seemed to be slightly more popular.

Some studies have yielded slightly different results. For example, in studying the role of sports as a social status determinant for children, Chase and Dummer had a total of 227 boys and 251 girls in grades 4, 5, and 6 complete a questionnaire to determine which criteria were most important in determining personal, female, and male popularity.[2] Personal popularity was answered by the girls and boys according to, "What would make you well liked by your classmates?" Female and male popularity was determined by asking both boys and girls to answer, "What would make (girls, for female subjects/boys, for male subjects) well liked by your classmates?" Boys revealed that sports have become more important and academic achievement less important in determining personal popularity. Boys reported sports to be the most important determinant of personal and male popularity and appearance as the most important determinant of female popularity. Sports and appearance became more important for boys with each higher grade level. Girls reported appearance to the most important determinant of personal, male and female popularity.

For girls, appearance also became more important with each higher grade level.

Admittedly, sociality and children's sports is difficult to study objectively, and this may be a part of the reason why so little research has been undertaken. This should not be interpreted to mean that sports experiences have little to contribute to social development of children, however. On the contrary, the potential value of sports in making positive contributions to social development are tremendous.

SOCIAL NEEDS

It is a relatively easy matter to identify specific components of physical fitness, but this does not necessarily hold true for components of social fitness. Thus, in the absence of definitive components of social fitness, other directions need to be pursued in our efforts to help children achieve satisfactory levels of social fitness.

Social maturity and social fitness may be expressed in terms of fulfillment of certain social needs. If social needs are being adequately met, the child should be in a better position to realize social fitness and achieve social development. Among the general needs we should give consideration to are (1) *the need for affection,* which involves acceptance and approval of persons; (2) *the need for belonging,* which involves acceptance and approval of the group; and (3) *the need for mutuality,* which involves cooperation, mutual helpfulness, and group loyalty. The conditions for meeting these needs are inherent in many sports experiences.

In addition to these general needs, the following lists reflect the developmental characteristics needed at different age levels.

Five-Year-Old Children

1. Interested in neighborhood games that involve any number of children
2. Play various games to test their skills
3. Enjoy other children and like to be with them
4. Interests largely self-centered
5. Seem to get along best in small groups
6. Show an interest in home activities

7. Imitate when playing
8. Get along well in taking turns
9. Respect the belongings of other people

Six-Year-Old Children

1. Self-centered and have need for praise
2. Like to be first
3. Indifferent of sex distinction
4. Enjoy group play when groups tend to be small
5. Like parties but behavior may not always be decorous
6. Most enjoy school association, have a desire to learn
7. Interests in conduct of friends
8. Boys like to fight and wrestle with peers to prove masculinity
9. Show an interest in group approval

Seven-Year-Old Children

1. Want recognition for individual achievements
2. Sex differences not of great importance
3. Not always good losers
4. Conversation often about family
5. Learning to stand up for own rights
6. Interested in friends and not influenced by their social or economic status
7. May have nervous habits such as nail biting, tongue sucking, scratching, or pulling at ear
8. Attaining orientation in time
9. Get greater enjoyment from group play
10. Show greater signs of cooperative efforts

Eight-Year-Old Children

1. Girls careful of their clothes; boys are not
2. Leave many things uncompleted
3. Have special friends
4. Have longer periods of peaceful play
5. Do not like playing alone
6. Enjoy dramatizing
7. Start collections

8. Enjoy school and dislike staying home
9. Like variety
10. Recognition of property rights is well established
11. Respond well to group activity
12. Interests in friends of own sex
13. Beginning of the desire to become a member of a club

Nine-Year-Old Children

1. Want to be like others, talk like others, and look like others
2. Girls becoming more interested in their clothes
3. Are generally conformists and may be afraid of that which is different
4. Able to be on their own
5. Able to be fairly responsible and dependable
6. Developing some firm and loyal friendships
7. Increasing development of qualities of leaders and followers
8. Increasing interest in activities involving challenges and adventure
9. Increasing participation in varied and organized group activities

Ten-Year-Old Children

1. Begin to recognize the fallibility of adults
2. Moving more into a peer-centered society
3. Amazingly self-dependent
4. Increased self-reliance; intensified group feelings
5. Widening divergence between the two sexes
6. Great team loyalties developing
7. Beginning to identify with their social contemporaries of the same sex
8. Relatively easy to appeal to their reason
9. On the whole, they have a fairly critical sense of justice
10. Boys show their friendship with other boys by wrestling and jostling with each other, and girls walk together with arms around each other as friends

11. Increased interest in people, in the community, and in affairs of the world
12. Interested in social problems in an elementary way and like to take part in discussion

Eleven-Year-Old Children

1. Internal guiding standards set up; although guided by what is done by other children, they will modify behavior in line with their own standards
2. Do a number of socially acceptable things, not because they are right or wrong
3. Although obsessed by standards of peers, are anxious for social approval of adults
4. Need for social companionship of children their own age
5. Increased interest in organized games
6. Girls likely self-conscious in presence of boys; usually much more mature than boys
7. Team spirit very strong
8. Boys' and girls' interests not always the same; may be some antagonism between the sexes
9. Often engage in silly behavior, such as giggling and clowning
10. Girls more interested in social appearance than boys are

Twelve-Year-Old Children

1. Increasing identification of self with other children of their own sex
2. Increasing recognition of fallibility of adults
3. May see themselves as children and adults as adults
4. Getting ready to make the difficult transition to adolescence
5. Pressure is being placed on them to begin to assume adult responsibilities

GUIDELINES FOR SOCIAL DEVELOPMENT THROUGH SPORTS

Guidelines for social development are set forth in the same manner that guidelines for physical development through sports were; that is, these guidelines take the form of valid *concepts of social develop-*

ment. When we have some basis for social behavior of children as they grow and develop we are then in a better position to select and conduct sports activities that are likely to be compatible with social development. The following list of concepts of social development with implications for children's sports discusses this.

1. *Interpersonal relationships are based on social needs.* All children should be given an equal opportunity in sports participation. Moreover, the coach should impress upon children their importance to the team. This can be done in connection with the team or group effort, which is so essential to successful participation. It is encouraging that some baseball leagues have a rule that every child must play and that every player must play in the infield at least part of the time.

2. *Children can develop their self-concept through undertaking roles.* Children are more likely to be aware of their particular abilities if given the opportunity to play different positions on a team. Rotation of such responsibilities as team captain tends to provide opportunity for self-expression of children through role-playing.

3. *There are various degrees of interaction between individuals and groups.* The sports experience should provide an outstanding setting for children to develop interpersonal interaction. The coach has the opportunity to observe them in action rather than in sedentary situations only. Consequently, the coach is in a good position to guide integrative experiences by helping children to see the importance of satisfactory interrelationships in sports group situations.

4. *Choosing and being chosen—an expression of a basic need—is a foundation of interpersonal relationships.* As often as possible, children should be given the opportunity for choosing teammates, partners, etc. However, great caution should be taken by the coach to see that this is carried out in an equitable way. At practice sessions the coach should devise methods of choosing so that certain children are not always selected last or left out entirely.

5. *Language is a basic means and essential accompaniment of socialization.* Children can be taught the language of the body through using the names of its parts as they participate in sports. For example, "Good arm, Jane," or "Put some foot into it, Joe." This is an important dimension in the development of body awareness. (This will be discussed in greater detail in Chapter 9.) Sports experiences should be such that there is opportunity for oral expression among and between children.

6. *Learning to play roles is a process of social development.* Children may be given the opportunity to play as many roles as possible in the sports experience. This could involve the organization and administration of sports activities such as selection of activities, making rules of play, and helping others with skills. Doing a physical skill is in itself the playing of a role, such as being a better thrower, catcher, etc. Thus, the very medium of sports activities is the process of social adjustment.

7. *Integrative interaction tends to promote social development.* The key word in this process to promote social development is *action,* which is the basis for sports participation. Sports participation is unique in its potential to accomplish integrative interaction, and thus promote social development. Spontaneity can be considered as one of the desired outcomes of integrative experiences, which means the opportunity for actions and feelings expressed by children as they really are. Active play is perhaps the most important aspect of life for children and, thus, spontaneous actions and feelings are best expressed through physical activity.

8. *Resistance to domination is an active attempt to maintain integrity.* The coach might consider resistance as a possible indicator of coach domination. If this occurs, the coach might look into his or her actions, which may be dominating the sports teaching-learning situation. Child resistance should be interpreted as a sign of a healthful personality, and a wise coach will likely be able to direct the energy into constructive channels to promote social development. A very natural outlet for this frustrated energy is found in desirable activities presented in a sports program.

9. *Interpersonal interaction between children is a basis for choice.* If children are left out by other children, this symptom should be studied with care to see if this is an indication of poor interpersonal relationships with other children. Very interesting aspects of interpersonal relationships can be observed by the wise coach. Children may realize the value of a child to a specific activity and accept such a child accordingly. On the other hand, they may be likely to accept their friends regardless of ability in sports skills.

10. *Children in and as a result of belonging to groups develop differently than they would as individuals alone.* Most sports activities provide an outstanding opportunity for children to engage actively in group experiences. Merely being a member of a team can be a most

rewarding experience for a child. If properly conducted, sports activities should provide an optimal situation for desirable social development because children focus their greatest personal interest in active play.

POSSIBILITIES FOR SOCIAL DEVELOPMENT THROUGH SPORTS

It has been suggested that the sports "laboratory" should present near-ideal surroundings and environment for the social development of children. It has also been indicated that coaches believe this area provides some of the best means for teaching vital social skills. In fact, the American Sports Education Program has proclaimed that participation in sports "develops social skills with other children and adults such as taking turns and sharing playing time."[3]

There are numerous sports situations through which children may gain a better understanding of the importance of cooperation. By their very nature, many games depend upon the cooperation of group members in achieving a common goal. In skills such as throwing and catching there must be a coordinated action of the thrower and catcher. In certain kinds of gymnastic activities, children participate and learn together in groups of three—two children assisting the performer and the others taking turns in performing. In these and countless other situations the importance of cooperating together for the benefit of the individual and the group is readily discerned.

In this regard, the following study by Berlage is of interest.[4] This researcher studied the similarities between children's competitive team sports and the typical corporate or business environment. Two research questions were posed: (1) Does the structural organization of children's soccer and ice hockey organizations resemble that of American corporations? and (2) Are the values of children's competitive sports similar to corporate values? Questionnaires were distributed to 222 Connecticut and New York fathers of eleven- or twelve-year-old sons on soccer and ice hockey teams. Through observations and interviews, it was found that the structural organizations of the children's ice hockey and soccer programs clearly resembled those of corporations. An organizational chart illustrated the hierarchies and divisions in a youth soccer program, and it was also found that the values stressed in competitive sports are similar to corporate values. The fathers selected teamwork (cooperation) as the most important sports attribute that would contribute to success in business. The importance of learning to be a part of a team was a constant theme in the fathers' responses. Although some fathers expressed misgivings about the amount of politics in the team selection process and the inconveniencies of complying with practice and travel schedules, most had positive attitudes toward competitive youth sports. It was concluded that those who have participated in competitive sports have an advantage over others who are not socialized in these values, skills, and attitudes.

Issues that come up as a result of certain misunderstandings in sports activities give rise to the exercise of wholesome social controls. The relationships of these controls in sports experiences to those in community living are understood in varying degrees by children at the different age levels. In these situations, outstanding settings are provided for the development of problem-solving techniques in which children are placed to make value judgments.

Some coaches have observed that while sports provide opportunities to encourage interpersonal communication and understanding among children, these opportunities are occasionally manifested in the form of minor conflicts. A procedure used to help solve such conflicts is called the "talking bench," on which two children sit until they have agreed upon the origin of their conflict and resolve it to the satisfaction of both.

The previous discussion included only a few of the numerous possibilities for social control, social interaction, and social development that are likely to be inherent in the sports experience. Admittedly, this does not accrue automatically, and any degree of success in social development through sports rests heavily upon the adults involved in children's sports.

EVALUATING CONTRIBUTIONS OF SPORTS TO SOCIAL DEVELOPMENT

It has been mentioned that coaches place great store in the contributions of sports to social development of children. It has also been suggested that little solid scientific evidence is available to support this belief. This makes it all the more important that coaches and parents as well critically examine those sports experiences that are being provided for children.

Processes for Evaluating Social Development in Sports

In the past, most of what has been done in this area has been of a subjective nature. The process of "observation" has been considered satisfactory because it has been felt that for the most part we can merely watch children to see the kinds of relationships that exist among them.

In recent years, I have approached this problem from a more scientific standpoint, using certain *sociometric techniques* with varying degrees of success. Included among such techniques are (1) sociograms, (2) sociographs, and (3) social distance scales.

Sociograms

In this technique, a child is usually asked to name in order of preference those persons liked best on a team. In the sports situation, a child may be asked to name those he or she would like to be with or play with most. After the choices are made, the results are plotted on a sociogram. If two children choose each other, they are known as "mutual choices of pairs." Those not selected by anyone in the group and who do not choose anyone are called "isolates." "Islands" is the name given to pairs or small groups of mutual choices not selected by any in the large group. Although the sociogram is a worthwhile device for identifying certain aspects of interpersonal relationships, it is a time-consuming procedure and for this reason is not one of the more popular methods used.

Sociographs

The sociograph is a more expedient and practical way of tabulating and interpreting data. Instead of plotting as in a sociogram, choices are recorded in tabular form opposite the names of children. This readily shows the number of rejections, mutual choices, choices received, and choices given.

Social Distance Scales

Social distance scales have been used in research in social psychology for over fifty years. In this procedure, each member of a group is asked to check the other members according to certain degrees of social intimacy such as:

1. I would like to have him or her as one of my friends.
2. I would like to have him or her on my team, but not as a close friend.
3. I would like to be with him or her once in awhile, but not often or for very long.
4. I do not mind his or her being on the team, but I do not want anything to do with him or her.
5. I wish he or she were not on the team.

This procedure can be used to determine the general social tone of a team. Team social distance scores on each individual child can be obtained by arbitrarily weighting the items previously listed. For example, if a child was checked two times for item number one ($2 \times 1 = 2$); six times for item two ($6 \times 2 = 12$); eight times for item three ($8 \times 3 = 24$); three times for item four ($3 \times 4 = 12$); and one time for item five ($1 \times 5 = 5$), the total score would be 55. (The lower the score, the greater the acceptance by the group and the less the social distance.) With this sample of twenty children, the lowest score would be 20 (20×1) and the highest score would be 100 (20×5).

These data can be used to determine, with some degree of objectivity, the extent to which the sports experience has contributed to social relationships; that is, the coach can compare scores before and after a group of children has been involved in a particular sports experience. This can be done on an individual game basis when a team has won or when it has lost. Also, it can be done at the beginning and at the end of an entire season to measure social growth, if any, that may have taken place among the participants.

I have used all of these sociometric techniques when I have been asked to make an assessment of a certain children's sports program. In some instances, the results have provided guidance in efforts to obtain a better understanding of social relationships and thus contribute to social development. It is recognized that most coaches are aware of those obvious factors concerned with group social structure. However, the many aspects of interpersonal relationships that are not so obvious are difficult to discern. It is the purpose of sociometric techniques to assist in the emergence of these relationships.

Sportsmanship

Any discussion about social development and sports would not be complete without some mention of sportsmanship. Sportsmanship is concerned with the social conduct of a participant who is thought of as a good loser and a gracious winner. In recent years, certain behaviors of participants and audiences as well have put a serious strain on what has been considered to be good sportsmanship. *Antisportsmanship* has been evident not only at the higher levels of sports participation but also in children's sports.

This condition prompted the NYSCA to conduct a summit on the subject. At this meeting Bob Bierscheid, chairman of the NYSCA National Board of Directors, indicated that the purpose for sponsoring this national summit was to help further define the National Standards for Youth Sports for youth leagues across America.[5] Further, the mission was to encourage every league to implement these standards.

To promote these aims, the NYSCA has produced the codes of ethics for coaches and parents that were mentioned in Chapter 4. Also, the association installed grievance procedures through which coaches may be decertified for behavior at odds with the association standards.

Participants at the NYSCA sportsmanship summit agreed that children enjoy sports most when they are taught and encouraged to sharpen their playing skills in an atmosphere of sportsmanship and fair play. My own studies tend to agree with this type of thinking.

Chapter 8

Emotional Development

At one time or another most everyone (children and adults alike) demonstrates emotional as well as ordinary behavior. Adults should not necessarily think in terms of always suppressing the emotions of children. On the contrary, the goal should be to help children express their emotions as harmlessly as possible when they do occur so that emotional stability will be maintained. If this can be accomplished, problems resulting from harmful emotional behavior can at least be reduced, if not eliminated entirely.

As mentioned in Chapter 1, emotional patterns can be arbitrarily placed into the two broad categories of pleasant and unpleasant emotions. Pleasant emotional patterns can include such feelings as joy, affection, happiness, and love, and unpleasant emotional patterns can include anger, sorrow, jealousy, fear, and worry. The pleasantness or unpleasantness of an emotion seems to be determined by its strength or intensity, by the nature of the situation arousing it, and by the way the child perceives or interprets the situation.

The ancient Greeks identified emotions with certain organs of the body. For example, sorrow was expressed from the heart (a broken heart), jealousy was associated with the liver, hate with the gallbladder, and anger with the spleen. In this regard, we sometimes hear the expression "venting your spleen" on someone. This historical reference is made because we have taken into account certain conduits between emotions and the body. These are by way of the nervous system and the endocrine system. The part of the nervous system principally concerned with the emotions is the *autonomic* nervous system, which controls functions such as heartbeat, blood pressure, and digestion. When there is a stimulus of any of the emotional patterns, these two systems activate. By way of illustration, if the emotional pattern of fear is stimulated, the heartbeat accelerates, breathing is more rapid, and blood pressure is likely to rise. Energy fuel is discharged into the bloodstream from storage in the liver, which causes sugar levels to rise. These help prepare a person for coping with the condition caused by the fear.

In the brief discussion of emotion in Chapter 5, it was suggested that the emotional objective of sports should imply that sympathetic guidance should be provided in meeting anxieties, joys, and sorrows, and help given in developing aspirations and security. In order to attempt to reach this objective, consider the standpoint of a growing child in terms of maturing emotionally.

For purposes of this discussion, I will consider maturity as being concerned with a state of readiness on the part of the organism. The term is most frequently used in connection with age relationships. For example, it may be said that "Johnny is mature for six years of age." Simply stated, emotional maturity is the process of acting your age.

Generally speaking, emotional maturity will be achieved through a gradual accumulation of mild and pleasant emotions. On the contrary, emotional immaturity indicates that unpleasant emotions have accumulated too rapidly for the individual to absorb. In order to pursue a sensible course in helping the child become more emotionally mature, certain factors need to be taken into account.

FACTORS CONCERNING EMOTIONAL DEVELOPMENT

Some of the factors concerned with emotional development are (1) characteristics of childhood emotionality, (2) emotional arousals and reactions, and (3) factors that influence emotionality.

Characteristics of Childhood Emotionality

1. *Ordinarily the emotions of children are not long-lasting.* A child's emotions may last for a few minutes or less and then terminate rather abruptly. The child gets it "out of his or her system" by expressing it outwardly. In contrast, some adult emotions may be long and drawn out. As children get older, expressing the emotions by overt action is encumbered by certain social restraints. This is to say that what might be socially acceptable at one age level is not necessarily so at another. This may be a reason for some children developing moods, which in a sense are states of emotion drawn out over a

period of time and expressed slowly. Typical moods of childhood may be that of "sulking" due to restraint of anger, being "jumpy" from repressed fear, and becoming "humorous" from controlled joy or happiness.

2. *The emotions of children are likely to be intense.* This might be confusing to some adults who do not understand child behavior; that is, they may not be able to see why children react rather strongly to situations that to them might appear insignificant.

3. *The emotions of children are subject to rapid change.* Children are capable of shifting rapidly from laughing to crying, or from anger to joy. Although the reason for this is not definitely known, it might be that there is not as much depth of feeling among children as there is among adults. In addition, it could be due to the lack of experience that children have had as well as their state of intellectual development. We do know that young children have a short attention span, which could cause them to change rapidly from one kind of emotion to another.

4. *The emotions of children can appear with a high degree of frequency.* As children get older, they acquire more experience with various kinds of emotional situations, and they develop the ability to adjust to situations that previously would have caused an emotional reaction. Perhaps children learn through experience what is socially acceptable and what is socially unacceptable. This is particularly true if children are reprimanded in some way following a strong emotional reaction. For this reason, children may try to confront situations in ways that do not involve an emotional response.

5. *Children differ in their emotional responses.* One child confronted with a situation that instills fear may run away from the immediate environment, and another might just stand there and cry. Different reactions of children to emotional situations are probably due to a host of factors. Included among these may be past experiences with certain kinds of emotional experiences, willingness of parents and other adults to help children become independent, and family relationships in general.

6. *Strength of children's emotions are subject to change.* At some age levels certain kinds of emotions may be weak and later become stronger. Conversely, with some children, emotions that were strong may tend to decline. For example, very young children may be timid

among strangers, but later when they see there is nothing to fear, the timidity is likely to wane.

Emotional Arousals and Reactions

If we are to understand the emotions of children, we need to take into account those factors of emotional arousal and how children might be expected to react to them. Many different kinds of emotional patterns have been identified. For purposes here, I have arbitrarily selected for discussion the emotional states of fear, worry, anger, jealousy, and joy.

1. *Fear.* It is possible that it is not necessarily the arousal itself but rather the way something is presented that determines whether there will be a fear reaction. For example, in a practice session if there is a discussion of a certain gymnastic activity in terms of "If you do it that way, you will break your neck," it is possible that a fear response will occur. This is one of the many reasons for using a positive approach, especially in the area of sports activities.

Children may react to fear by withdrawing. With very young children this may be in the form of crying or breath holding. With children under the age of three, and in some older children as well, the "ostrich" approach may be used; that is, children may hide their faces in order to get away from it. As children get older, these forms of reaction may decrease or cease altogether because of social pressures. For instance, it may be considered "sissy" to cry, especially among boys. (The validity of this kind of thinking is, of course, open to question.)

In my studies the three greatest fears children have about sports are (1) getting hurt, (2) losing, and (3) not playing well.

2. *Worry.* This might be considered an imaginary form of fear, and it can be a fear not aroused directly from the child's environment. Worry can be aroused by imagining a situation that could possibly arise; that is, a child could worry about not being able to perform well in a certain sports situation. Since worries are likely to be caused by imaginary rather than real conditions, they are not likely to be found in abundance among very young children. Perhaps the reason for this is that they have not reached a stage of intellectual development where they imagine certain things that could cause worry. Although children will respond to worry in different ways, certain manifestations such as nail biting may be symptomatic of this condition.

3. *Anger.* This emotional response tends to occur more frequently than fear. This is probably due to the fact that there are more conditions that incite anger. In addition, some children quickly learn that anger may get attention that otherwise would not be forthcoming. It is likely that as children get older they may show more anger responses than fear responses because they soon see that there is not too much to fear.

Anger is caused by many factors, one of which is interference with the movements the child wants to execute. This interference can come from others or by the child's own limitations in ability and physical development. This, of course, can be an important factor in the performance of certain tasks in sports.

Because of individual differences in children, there is a wide variation in anger responses. In general, these responses are either *impulsive* or *inhibited.* In impulsive responses, children manifest an overt action either toward another person or an object that caused the anger. For instance, a child who collides with a door might take out the anger by hitting or kicking the door. (This form of behavior is also sometimes manifested by some "adults.") Inhibited responses are likely to be kept under control, and as children mature emotionally they acquire more ability to control their anger.

My studies show that the three greatest causes of anger among children when they participate in sports are (1) when some players cheat, (2) when someone plays dirty, and (3) getting yelled at.

4. *Jealousy.* This response usually occurs when children fear a threat of loss of affection. Many psychologists believe that jealousy is closely related to anger. Because of this, children may build up resentment against other people. Jealousy can be very devastating in childhood, and every effort should be made to avoid it.

Jealousy is concerned with social interaction that involves people children like. These individuals can be parents, siblings, teachers, coaches, and peers. There are various ways in which children may respond. These include (1) being aggressive toward the one they are jealous of, or possibly toward others as well; (2) withdrawing from the person whose affections they think have been lost; and (3) possible development of an "I don't care" attitude.

In some cases children will not respond in any of these ways. They might try to excel over the person of whom they are jealous. In other words, they may tend to do things to impress the person whose affections they thought have been lost.

5. *Joy.* This pleasant emotion is one that we strive for because it is so important in maintaining emotional stability. Causes of joy differ from one age level to another and from one child to another. This is to say that what might be a joyful situation for one person may not necessarily be so for another.

Joy is expressed in various ways, but the most common are laughing and smiling, the latter being a restrained form of laughter. Some people respond to joy with a state of body relaxation. This is difficult to detect because it has little or no overt manifestation. However, it may be noticed when compared to body tension caused by unpleasant emotions.

My studies show that a large majority of children derive the joyful experience of fun from participating in sports. The next three experiences of joy from sports are (1) keeping fit, (2) winning, and (3) team spirit.

EMOTIONAL NEEDS

It has been mentioned that it is easy to identify specific components of physical fitness. This does not hold true for social fitness, and neither does it hold true for emotional fitness. Therefore, in the absence of definitive components of emotional fitness, we need to look in other directions in our efforts to help children maintain satisfactory levels of emotional fitness.

Emotional maturity, and, hence, emotional fitness, could be expressed in terms of the fulfillment of certain emotional needs. These needs can be reflected in the developmental characteristics of growing children. A number of emotional characteristics are identified in the following lists.

Five-Year-Old Children

1. Seldom show jealousy toward younger siblings
2. Usually see only one way to do something
3. Usually see only one answer to a question
4. Want to be more independent

5. Reach for new experiences and try to relate to enlarged world
6. Overanxious to reach goals set by parents and teachers
7. Critical of self and sensitive to failure
8. Emotional pattern of anger more controlled
9. Becoming more impulsive and boisterous in actions than at six

Six-Year-Old Children

1. Restless and may have difficulty in making decisions
2. Emotional pattern of anger difficult to control at times
3. Behavior patterns often explosive and unpredictable
4. Jealous toward siblings at times; at other times take pride in siblings
5. Greatly excited by anything new
6. Behavior susceptible to shifts in direction, inwardly motivated, and outwardly stimulated
7. May be self-assertive and dramatic

Seven-Year-Old Children

1. Curiosity and creative desires may condition responses
2. May be difficult to take criticism from adults
3. Develop sympathy and loyalty to others
4. Do not mind criticism or punishment if believing it to be fair, but are indignant if they think it unfair
5. Disdainful of danger to safety and self, which may be a result of increasing interest in activities involving challenges and adventure

Eight-Year-Old Children

1. Dislike taking much criticism from adults
2. Can give and take criticism in own group
3. May develop enemies
4. Do not like to be treated as children
5. Have marked sense of humor
6. First impulse is to blame others
7. Become more realistic and want to find out for themselves

Nine-Year-Old Children

1. May sometimes be outspoken and critical of the adults they know, although there is a genuine fondness for them
2. Respond best to adults when treated as individuals and they approach them in an adult way
3. Like recognition for what they have done and respond well to deserved praise
4. Likely to be backward about public recognition but like private praise
5. Inclined not to change plans in the middle of an activity, but would rather begin over
6. May fear being deprived of mother
7. Some definite personality traits evidenced
8. Are learning to get along better, but still may resort to quarreling and fighting
9. Like to be trusted with errands
10. Enjoy performing simple tasks
11. Want to please and do what is expected of them
12. Are beginning to sense right and wrong in terms of specific situations

Ten-Year-Old Children

1. Increasing tendency to rebel against adult domination
2. Capable of loyalties and hero worship, and can inspire it in their schoolmates
3. Can be readily inspired to group loyalties in their club organization
4. Like the sense of solidarity that comes from keeping a group secret as a member of a group
5. Each sex has an increasing tendency to show lack of sympathy and understanding with the other
6. Boys' and girls' behaviors and interests increasingly different

Eleven-Year-Old Children

1. If unskilled in group games, may tend to withdraw
2. Boys may be concerned if they feel underdeveloped
3. May appear indifferent and uncooperative

4. Moods change quickly
5. Want to grow up but may be afraid to leave childhood security behind
6. Increase in self-direction and in a serious attitude toward work
7. Need for approval to feel secure
8. Beginning to have a fully developed idea of own importance

Twelve-Year-Old Children

1. Beginning to develop a truer picture of morality
2. Clearer understanding of real causal relations
3. Sexual maturation involves structural and physiological changes and possible perplexing and disturbing emotional problems
4. Personal appearance a source of great conflict, and learning to appreciate good grooming or the reverse may be prevalent
5. May be very easily hurt when criticized or made the scapegoat
6. Maladjustment may occur when there is not a harmonious relationship between them and adults

GUIDELINES FOR EMOTIONAL DEVELOPMENT THROUGH SPORTS

Guidelines for emotional development are set forth here in the same manner that guidelines for physical and social development through sports were proposed in the two previous chapters; that is, these guidelines take the form of valid *concepts of emotional development*. When we have a basis for the emotional behavior of children as they grow and develop, we are then in a better position to provide sports experiences that are likely to be compatible with emotional development. The following list of concepts of emotional development with implications for children's sports discusses this.

1. *An emotional response may be brought about by a goal being furthered or thwarted.* The coach should make a very serious effort to assure successful sports experiences for every child. This can be accomplished in part by attempting to provide for individual differences within given sports experiences. The sports setting should be

such that each child derives a feeling of personal worth through making some sort of positive contribution.

2. *Self-realization experiences should be constructive.* The opportunity for creative experience inherent in sports affords children an excellent chance for self-realization through physical expression. Coaches might consider planning with children themselves to see that activities are meeting their needs and, as a result, involve a constructive experience.

3. *Emotional responses increase as the development of children brings greater awareness, including the ability to remember the past and to anticipate the future.* The coach can remind the children of their past emotional responses with words of praise. This should encourage them to repeat such responses in future similar sports situations.

4. *As children develop, their emotional reactions tend to become more discriminating.* A well-planned and progressive sequence of sports experiences can provide for release of aggression in a socially acceptable manner.

5. *Emotional reactions displayed in early childhood are likely to be continued in some form in later years.* This could be one of the best reasons for providing sports experiences for children. Through sports experiences in the formative years we can help children develop constructive emotional reactions through a medium that they understand best body movement. Through the spontaneous freedom of expression of emotional reactions in the sports experience, the real feelings of children are more easily identified.

6. *Emotional reactions tend to increase beyond normal expectancy toward the constructive or destructive on the balance of furthering or hindering experiences of children.* For some children, the confidence they need to be able to face the problems of life may come about through sports. Therefore, sports have tremendous potential to help contribute toward a solid base for total development.

7. *Depending on certain factors, a child's own feelings may be accepted or rejected by the individual.* Children's sports experiences should make them feel good and have confidence in themselves. Satisfactory self-concept is closely related to body control; therefore, sports experiences might be considered as one of the best ways of contributing to it.

OPPORTUNITIES FOR EMOTIONAL
DEVELOPMENT THROUGH SPORTS

Coaches praise sports for their potential to provide emotional stability. The extent to which this actually accrues is dependent primarily upon the kind of emotional climate provided by the coach and the sports experiences provided for the children. For this reason it appears pertinent to examine some of the opportunities that exist for emotional development through sports.

1. *Release of aggression in a socially acceptable manner.* This is an outstanding way in which sports experiences can help to make children more secure and emotionally stable. For example, kicking a ball in a game of soccer or hitting a baseball can afford a socially acceptable way of releasing aggression.

2. *Inhibition of direct response of unpleasant emotions.* This does not necessarily mean that feelings concerned with such unpleasant emotions as fear and anger should be completely restrained. On the contrary, the interpretation should be that such feelings can take place less frequently in a good sports situation. This means that opportunities can be provided to relieve tension rather than aggravate it.

3. *Promotion of pleasant emotions.* Perhaps there is too much concern with suppressing unpleasant emotions and not enough attention given to the promotion of pleasant ones. One of the glorious things about sports is that the range of activities is so great that there is "something for everybody." Thus, all children, regardless of ability, should be afforded the opportunity for success, at least some of the time.

4. *Freedom from fear.* This largely depends upon the approach taken by the coach. As mentioned previously, when discussing a gymnastic activity, if the coach says, "If you do it that way, you will break your neck," such a negative approach can instill a fear that may not have existed originally. Remember that getting hurt is a fear that many children and parents have about sports.

5. *Recognition of abilities and limitations.* It has been mentioned that the wide range of activities in sports as well as different positions played should provide an opportunity for success for all. This should make it easier to provide for individual differences of children so that all of them can progress within the limits of their own skills and abilities.

6. *Understanding about the ability and achievement of others.* In the sports experience, emphasis can be placed upon the achievement of the group along with the function of each individual in the group. Team play is the basis of many sports activities.

7. *Being able to make a mistake without being ostracized.* This requires that the coach serve as a catalyst who helps children understand the idea of trial and error. Emphasis can be placed on "trying" and that they can learn not only from their own mistakes but from the mistakes of others as well.

The previous discussion includes just a few examples of the numerous opportunities to help provide for emotional development through sports. The resourceful and creative coach will be able to expand this list manyfold. It bears repeating that emotional development through sports will not accrue automatically. Although sports theoretically provide a near-ideal setting for children to act in terms of ordinary behavior instead of highly emotional behavior, this situation does not always prevail. For instance, in cases where children are placed under stress in highly competitive situations over prolonged periods, there may be a strong possibility of detraction from, rather than a contribution to, their emotional stability.

EVALUATING CONTRIBUTIONS OF SPORTS
TO EMOTIONAL DEVELOPMENT

When we attempt to evaluate the emotional aspect of personality, we tend to encounter much the same situation as when we attempt to evaluate the social aspect. Included among some of the methods used for attempting to measure emotional responses are the following:

1. Blood pressure (it rises when a person is under emotional stress)
2. Blood sugar analysis (under stressful conditions more sugar enters the bloodstream)
3. Pulse rate (emotional stress causes it to elevate)
4. Galvanic skin response (similar to the lie detector technique, and measurements are recorded in terms of perspiration in palms of hands)

These as well as others that have been used by investigators of human emotion have various and perhaps limited degrees of validity. In attempting to assess emotional reactivity, we oftentimes encounter the problem of the extent to which we are dealing with a purely physiological response or a purely emotional response. For example, a person's pulse rate could be elevated through some sort of physical exercise. It could likewise be elevated if he or she were the object of an embarrassing remark by another person. Thus, in this illustration the elevation of pulse rate could be caused by different reasons; the first being physiological and the second emotional.

I can also illustrate this with an experiment that I conducted several years ago. At the time I was proclaiming that the game of golf was much more emotional than physical: that is, "You can't raise a pulse rate with a putt." I had ten sixth-grade boys stand around the edge of a large green to see which one could "get down" in the least number of strokes. Pulse rates were taken just before and after the activity. For most of the boys there was little or no rise in pulse rate. The next step was to offer a prize of one dollar to the winner. Pulse rates were again taken for each boy and a considerable rise occurred. By introducing the "emotional variable," I was able to show the difference between a purely physiological response and a purely emotional one.

Another consideration to take into account is that the type of emotional pattern is not identified by the measuring device; that is, a joy response and an anger response could show the same or nearly the same rise in pulse rate. These are some of the reasons that it is most difficult to arrive at a high degree of objectivity in studying the emotional aspect of personality.

What we are essentially concerned with here is how an individual coach can make some sort of valid evaluation of the extent to which sports contribute to emotional development. This means that the coach should make some attempt to assess sports experiences with reference to whether these experiences provide emotional maturity.

One such approach would be to refer back to the list of opportunities for emotional development through sports suggested earlier in this chapter. I have converted these opportunities into a rating scale as follows:

1. The sports experience provides for release of aggression in a socially acceptable manner.
   4   most of the time
   3   some of the time

    2 occasionally
    1 infrequently
2. The sports experience provides for inhibition of direct response of unpleasant emotions.
    4 most of the time
    3 some of the time
    2 occasionally
    1 infrequently
3. The sports experience provides for promotion of pleasant emotions.
    4 most of the time
    3 some of the time
    2 occasionally
    1 infrequently
4. The sports experience provides for freedom from fear.
    4 most of the time
    3 some of the time
    2 occasionally
    1 infrequently
5. The sports experience provides for recognition of abilities and limitations.
    4 most of the time
    3 some of the time
    2 occasionally
    1 infrequently
6. The sports experience provides for an understanding about the ability and achievement of others.
    4 most of the time
    3 some of the time
    2 occasionally
    1 infrequently
7. The sports experience provides for being able to make a mistake without being ostracized.
    4 most of the time
    3 some of the time
    2 occasionally
    1 infrequently

If these ratings are made objectively and conscientiously, a reasonably good procedure for evaluation is provided. Ratings can be made periodically to see if positive changes are taking place. Ratings can be made for a single sports experience, a group of sports experiences, or for an entire season. This procedure can help the coach and parent identify the extent to which sports experiences and/or conditions under which the experiences take place are contributing to emotional development.

Chapter 9

Intellectual Development

Intellectual development of children through sports has been subjected to a great deal of criticism by some. It has been demonstrated, however, that there are many potential opportunities for intellectual development through the medium of sports.

INTELLECTUAL NEEDS

In Chapter 1, the point was made that children have certain intellectual needs: (1) a need for challenging experiences at the child's level of ability, (2) a need for intellectually successful and satisfying experiences, (3) a need for the opportunity to solve problems, and (4) a need for the opportunity to participate in creative experiences instead of always having to conform. These specific needs can be reflected in the developmental characteristics of children. The following lists identify a number of these characteristics.

Five-Year-Old Children

1. Enjoy copying designs, letters, and numbers
2. Interested in completing tasks
3. May tend to monopolize table conversation
4. Memory for past events good
5. Look at books and pretend to read
6. Like recordings, words, and music that tell a story
7. Enjoy counting objects
8. Over 2,000 words in speaking vocabulary
9. Can speak in complete sentences
10. Can sing simple melodies, beat good rhythms, and recognize simple tunes

11. Daydreams involve make-believe play
12. Attention span increasing up to twenty minutes in some cases
13. Are able to plan activities
14. Enjoy stories, dramatic plays, and poems
15. Enjoy making up dances to music
16. Pronunciation usually clear
17. Can express needs well in words

Six-Year-Old Children

1. Speaking vocabulary is over 2,500 words
2. Attention span inclined to be short
3. Know number combinations up to ten
4. Know comparative values of coins
5. Can define objects in terms of what they are used for
6. Know the right and left sides of body
7. Have an association with creative activity and motorized life experience
8. Drawings crude but realistic and suggestive of early man
9. Will contribute to guided group planning
10. Conversation usually concerns own experience and interests
11. Curiosity is active and memory is strong
12. Identify themselves with imaginary characters

Seven-Year-Old Children

1. Abstract thinking is barely beginning
2. Are able to listen longer
3. Read some books by themselves
4. Are able to reason, but have little experience upon which to base judgments
5. Attention span still short and retention poor, but they do not object to repetition
6. Reaction time still slow
7. Learning to evaluate the achievements of themselves and others
8. Concerned with their own lack of skill and achievement
9. Becoming more realistic and less imaginative

Eight-Year-Old Children

1. Can tell day of month and year
2. Voluntary attention span increasing
3. Interested in far-off places, and ways of communicating now have real meaning
4. Becoming more aware of adult world and their place in it
5. Ready to tackle almost anything
6. Show a capacity for self-evaluation
7. Like to memorize
8. Not always good at telling time, but very much aware of it

Nine-Year-Old Children

1. Individual differences clear and distinct
2. Some real interests beginning to develop
3. Beginning to have a strong sense of right and wrong
4. Understand explanations
5. Interests are closer to ten- or eleven-year-olds than to seven- or eight-year-olds
6. If a project fails to hold interest, it may be dropped without further thought
7. Attention span greatly increased
8. Seem to be guided best by a reason, simple and clear cut, for a decision that needs to be made
9. Ready to learn from occasional failure of their judgment as long as learning takes place in situations where failure will not have too serious consequences
10. Able to make up their own minds and come to decisions
11. Marked reading disabilities begin to be more evident and may tend to influence the personality
12. Wide range of interest in reading, in that many are great readers and others may be barely interested in books
13. Will average between six and seven words per remark

Ten-Year-Old Children

1. Work with executive speed and like the challenge of mathematics
2. Show a capacity to budget time and energy

3. Can attend to a visual task and at the same time maintain conversation
4. Some become discouraged and may give up trying when unsuccessful
5. The attention span has lengthened considerably, and they are able to listen, follow directions, and retain knowledge more easily
6. Beginning understanding of real causal relations
7. Making finer conceptual distinctions and thinking reflectively
8. Developing a scientific approach
9. Better oriented with respect to time
10. Ready to plan the day and accept responsibility for getting things done on time

Eleven-Year-Old Children

1. Increasing power of attention
2. Able to maintain a longer period of intellectual activity between firsthand experiences
3. Interested in scientific experiments and procedures
4. Can carry on many individual intellectual responsibilities
5. Able to discuss problems and to see different side of questions
6. May lack maturity of judgment
7. Increased language facility
8. Attention span is increasing; concentration may be given to a task for a long period of time
9. Level of aspiration increased
10. Growing in ability to use several facts to make a decision
11. Insight into causal relationships is developing more and is manifested by many "how" and "why" questions

Twelve-Year-Old Children

1. Learn more ways of studying and controlling the physical world
2. The use of language (in many cases their own vocabulary) to exchange ideas for explanatory reasons
3. More use of reflective thinking and greater use of distinction
4. Continuation in development of scientific approach

GUIDELINES FOR INTELLECTUAL DEVELOPMENT THROUGH SPORTS

Guidelines for intellectual development are set forth here in the same manner that guidelines for physical, social, and emotional development through sports were proposed in previous chapters; that is, these guidelines take the form of valid *concepts of intellectual development.* When we have some sort of basis for intellectual behavior of children as they grow and develop, we are then in a better position to provide sports experiences that are likely to be compatible with intellectual development. The following list of concepts of intellectual development with implications for children's sports discusses this.

1. *Children differ in intelligence.* Coaches and parents should be aware that poor performance of some children in sports activities might be due to the fact that they have difficulty with communication. Differences in intelligence levels as well as physical skill and ability need to be taken into account in the planning of sports practice sessions.

2. *Intelligence develops through the interaction of children and their environment.* Body movement experiences in sports involve a process of interaction with the environment. There are many problem-solving opportunities in the well-planned sports environment, and thus children can be presented with challenging learning situations.

3. *Emotional stress may affect measures of intelligence.* Sports experiences have potential value in the relief of emotional stress. This can possibly make children more effective from an intellectual point of view.

4. *Extremes in intelligence show differences in personality characteristics.* The coach should be aware of the range of intelligence of children in a particular group. Experiences should be provided that challenge the so-called gifted child as well as meeting the needs of those children who are below average. In the sports experience, children can learn to respect individual differences as far as levels of intelligence are concerned.

5. *The children's abilities to deal with intellectual tasks influence their successful dealings with such tasks.* The sports experience should contain a large degree of variation (playing different positions on a team). This way it will likely ensure that all children will achieve success at one time or another.

OPPORTUNITIES FOR INTELLECTUAL
DEVELOPMENT THROUGH SPORTS

The idea that participation in sports can contribute to a child's intellectual development is not necessarily new. For example, more than twenty-three centuries ago Plato postulated in *The Republic:* "No compulsion my good friend . . . in teaching children, train them by a kind of game, and you will be able to see more clearly the natural bent of each." In her early twentieth-century book on games, Jessie H. Bancroft commented that, "As a child's perceptions are quickened, he sees more quickly that the ball is coming toward him, that he is in danger of being tagged, or that it is his turn. He hears footsteps behind him, or his name or number called; he feels the touch on the shoulder; or in innumerable ways he is aroused to the quick and direct recognition of, and response to, things that go on around him."[1]

Most learning theorists agree that problem solving is the major way of human learning; that is, learning can take place well when problem-solving opportunities are provided. In a well-planned sports situation there are numerous opportunities for children to exercise judgment and resort to reflective thinking in the solution of various kinds of problems. In addition, children must acquire a knowledge of rules and regulations for various games. It is also important for effective participation that they gain an understanding of the various fundamentals and strategies involved in the performance of sports activities.

Another very important aspect of intellectual development in sports is improving *listening* skills. In the auditory-input phase of a sports teaching-learning situation, children "attend to" better than they do in this phase of a lesson in school subject areas. This means that in a well-planned sports learning situation, the child's attention is likely to be focused on the learning task and learning behavior.

Improving Perceptual-Motor Development

Perception is concerned with how we obtain information from the environment through the various sensory modalities and what we make of it, and *motor* is concerned with the impulse for motion resulting in a change of position through the various forms of body movement. When the two terms are put together (perceptual-motor) the implication is an organization of interpretation of sensory data, with related voluntary motor responses.

Perceptual-motor development involves the correction or at least some degree of improvement of certain motor deficiencies, especially those associated with fine motor coordination. What some specialists have identified as a "perceptual-motor deficit" syndrome is said to exist with certain neurologically handicapped children. An attempt may be made to correct or improve fine motor control problems through a carefully developed sequence of motor competencies which follow a definite hierarchy of development. This may occur through a structured perceptual-motor program, which is likely to be dependent upon a series of systematic exercises. Or it can occur through participation in certain sports with attempts to provide for these corrections or improvements when children engage in sports activities where perceptual-motor developmental factors may be inherent. This procedure (sports participation) is much more fun for children and at the same time is more likely to be free from emotionally traumatizing situations sometimes attendant in some highly structured perceptual-motor programs.

Perceptual-Motor Skills

Child development specialists agree that there is no simple distinction between a perceptual skill and a motor skill. This has no doubt led to the term *perceptual-motor skills*. In fact, to some extent this term may have supplanted such terms as *neuromuscular* and *sensorimotor*.

In general, the postulation appears to be that if perceptual training improves perceptual and motor abilities, then, because of the fact that perceptual and motor abilities are so highly interrelated and interdependent upon each other, it follows that training in perception should alleviate perceptual-motor problems. There is objective support for the idea that perceptual training can improve perceptual ability. Although there is not a great deal of clear-cut evidence to support the idea that perceptual-motor training does increase the performance of perceptual-motor skills, some research has indicated that perceptual-motor skills can be significantly improved under certain conditions.

What then are the perceptual-motor skills? Generally, the kinds of skills that fit into a combination of manual coordination and eye-hand skills may be considered a valid classification.

Visual perception is based on sensorimotor experiences that depend on visual acuity, eye-hand coordination, left-right body orientation, and other visual spatial abilities including visual sequencing. Some studies have shown a positive correlation between difficulties in visual perception and achievement in reading.

Indications of a child's eye-hand coordination may be observed as he or she bounces or throws a ball. In reading, the child shows difficulty in eye-hand coordination by the inability to keep his or her place, to find the place once again in the pattern of printed words, and to maintain the motor adjustment as long as is necessary to comprehend a word, a phrase, or a sentence. His or her tendency to skip lines arises from an inability to direct the eyes accurately to the beginning of the next line.

Depending upon a variety of extenuating circumstances, perceptual-motor skills require a degree of voluntary action. The basic striking and catching skills are examples of this type and are important in certain kinds of team games; that is, receiving an object (catching) such as a ball, and hitting (striking) an object, ordinarily with an implement, such as batting a ball.

There are tasks perceptual-motor in character that are accomplished with one hand. At a high level of performance this could involve catching a ball with one hand in a highly organized sports activity such as baseball. At a very low level, a baby will reach for an object or grasp an object with one hand.

In some kinds of visual tasks requiring the use of one eye, there appears to be an eye preference. In reading, it is believed that one eye may lead or be dominant. In tasks where one eye is used and one hand is used, most people will use those on the same side of the body. This is to say that there is *lateral dominance*. In the case of those who use the left eye and right hand or the opposite of this, *mixed dominance* is said to exist. Some studies suggest that mixed dominance may have a negative effect on motor coordination; but just as many investigators report that this is not the case.

The development of perceptual-motor abilities in children is referred to by some child development specialists as the process of providing "learning to learn" activities. This means improvement upon such perceptual-motor qualities as body awareness, laterality and directionality (sense of direction), auditory and visual perception skills, and kinesthetic and tactile perception skills. A deficiency in one or more of these can detract from a child's ability to learn.

The following discussions will help adults determine whether such deficiencies exist, along with how participation in certain sports experiences help improve upon them. Even though a deficiency does not exist in any of these factors, the sports experiences suggested can still be used to sharpen and improve upon these skills that are so important to learning.

Body Image

The best description that I have seen of body image is that given by British sports psychologist H. T. A. Whiting and his associates several years ago. They described it as: "an appreciation and understanding of the body as an instrument of movement and vehicle of expression in nonverbal communication."[2]

It is doubtful that there are any foolproof methods of detecting problems of body image in children. The reason for this is that many mannerisms said to be indicative of body-image problems can be symptomatic of other deficiencies. Nevertheless, those adults who work with children should be alert to detect certain possible deficiencies. One way to detect body-image problems is to observe certain behaviors. The following list contains examples of such behavior.

1. Sometimes children with a lack of body image may manifest tenseness in their movements. At the same time they may be unsure of their movements in attempting to move the body segments.

2. If children are instructed to move a body part such as placing one foot forward, they may direct attention to the body part before making the movement. Or they may look at another child to observe the movement before attempting to make the movement. This could be due to poor processing of the input (auditory or visual) provided for the movement.

3. When instructed to use one body part (arm), children may also move the corresponding body part (other arm) when it is not necessary. For example, when asked to swing the right arm they may also start to swing the left arm simultaneously.
4. In such activities as catching a ball children may turn toward the ball when it is not necessary. For example, when a basketball comes close to them, they may move forward with either side of the body rather than trying to retrieve the ball with the hands as both feet remain stationary.

In general, when children are given the opportunity to use the body freely in enjoyable movement such as sports, an increase in body image occurs. In games that require running, such as football, baseball, basketball, and soccer, the importance of the feet and legs is recognized. Games that require use of the hands and arms are useful in the identification of the upper extremities. Thus, there are many opportunities in sports activities to improve upon body image.

Laterality and Directionality

Laterality and directionality are concerned with distinction of the body sides and sense of direction. More specifically, laterality is an internal awareness of the left and right sides of the body. It is concerned with the knowledge of how each side of the body is used separately or together. Directionality is the projection into space of laterality; that is, the awareness of left and right, up and down, over and under, etc. Stated in another way, directionality in space is the ability to project outside the body the laterality that children have developed within themselves.

The categories of laterality and directionality make up the broad classification of *directional awareness*. The development of this quality is most important in that it is an essential element for reading and writing. These two basic Rs require the hand and/or eyes to move from left to right in a coordinated manner. Also, interpretation of left and right direction is an important requirement for children in dealing with the environment. It is interesting to note that some children who have not developed laterality quite often will write numbers sequentially from left to right. However, when doing addition and subtraction they may want to start from the left instead of the right.

Since laterality and directionality are inherent aspects of body awareness, some of the methods of detecting deficiencies in body awareness mentioned previously apply here. In addition, it may be noted that children are inclined to use the dominant side of the body. Also, confusion may result if they are given directions for body movement that call for a specific direction in which they are to move.

In activities that require running to a given point such as a base, children may tend to veer away from it. Or they may not perceive the position of other children in a game such as basketball and, as a consequence, may run into them frequently. These are factors that adults can observe.

Generally speaking, a relatively large number of sports activities involve some aspect of lateralness, and a more moderate number are concerned with directionality. Some sports activities involve *unilateral* movements; those performed with one side or part of the body (throwing with the dominant arm). Some sports involve *bilateral* movement. This means that both sides or segments of the body are in action simultaneously in the same manner, such as the two-hand shot in basketball. *Cross-lateral* movement is involved when segments of the body are used simultaneously but in a different manner (running and dribbling a basketball). Many activities are concerned with changing direction that is likely to involve directionality (any sport that requires dodging).

Sometimes it is useful to engage in certain kinds of practice drills to provide for laterality and directionality, for example, the Zig-Zag Run. In this activity, a group is divided into teams. The teams form rows behind a starting line. Four tenpins or other objects are placed in a line four feet apart in front of each team. On a signal, the first child on each team runs to the right of the first pin and to the left of the second pin, and so on, in a zig-zag fashion, going around the last pin. The child returns to place in the same manner. The second child proceeds as the first did. If a child knocks down a pin, that child must set it up before continuing. The team that finishes first wins. This activity gives children practice in changing direction as they run around the objects. The adult can observe closely to notice the children who are having difficulty in performing the task. This practice can carry over into more complex sports activities that require dodging, as in the case of a forward trying to elude a guard in basketball.

Kinesthetic Perception

Kinesthesis has been described in many ways. Some definitions of the term are somewhat comprehensive and others are less so. One comprehensive definition of kinesthesis is that it is the sense that enables us to determine the position of the segments of the body, their rate, extent, and direction of movement, the position of the entire body, and the characteristics of total body motion. Another less-complicated definition of the term characterizes it as the sense that tells the individual where his or her body is and how it moves.

In summarizing the many definitions of the term the following four factors seem to be constant: (1) position of the body segments, (2) precision of movement, (3) balance, and (4) space orientation. For the discussion here, I will think of kinesthetic perception as the mental interpretation of the sensation of body movement.

Although a number of specific test items are supposed to measure kinesthesis, the use of such tests may be of questionable value in diagnosing deficiency in children. Therefore, my recommendation is that adults resort to the observation of certain behaviors and mannerisms of children, using some simple diagnostics to determine deficiencies in kinesthetic sensitivity.

Various authorities on the subject suggest that children with kinesthetic problems possess certain characteristics that may be identifying factors. For example, children who are deficient in kinesthetic sensitivity will likely be clumsy, awkward, and inefficient in their movements and impaired in getting acquainted with the handling of the world of objects. Children who have difficulty in the use of their hands or bodies in attempting to perform unfamiliar tasks involving body movement can no doubt benefit from activities involving kinesthesis.

Adults should be on the alert to observe children who have difficulty with motor coordination, that is, using the muscles in such a manner that they work together effectively. Such lack of coordination may be seen in children who have difficulty in performing the movement skills that involve an uneven rhythm such as skipping.

Since balance is an important aspect of kinesthesis, simple tests for balance are administered to determine if there is lack of proficiency. One such test is to have children stand on either foot. Ordinarily, they should be able to maintain such a position for a period of at least five seconds.

Since kinesthetic sensitivity is concerned with the sensation of movement and orientation of the body in space, it is not an easy matter to isolate specific activities suited only for this purpose. The reason for this, of course, is that practically all of these activities involve total or near-total physical response. However, activities that make children particularly aware of the movement of certain muscle groups, as well as those where resistance is encountered, are of particular value in helping them develop a kinesthetic awareness of their bodies. Many sports activities provide these qualities that will improve their kinesthetic sensitivity.

Rush and Tug can be used in practice sessions for sports activities to sharpen children's kinesthetic sensitivity. In this activity there are two groups, with each group standing next to one of two parallel lines that are about forty feet apart. In the middle of these two parallel lines is a rope laid perpendicular to them. A cloth is tied to the middle of the rope to designate the center of the rope. On a signal, members of both groups rush to their half of the rope, pick it up, and tug toward its own end line. The group pulling the midpoint of the rope past its own end line in a specified amount of time is the winner. If, at the end of a designated time, the midpoint of the rope has not been pulled beyond either group's line, the group with the midpoint of the rope closest to its end line is the winner. In this activity the children can be reminded of the resistance they are experiencing as they try to pull the opposing group as well as the experiences of feeling the muscle groups of the arms and legs working together.

Tactile Perception

The tactile sense is very closely related to the kinesthetic sense—so much so, in fact, that these two senses are often confused. One of the main reasons for this is that the ability to detect change in touch (tactile) involves many of the same receptors concerned with informing the body of changes in its position. The essential difference between the tactile sense and the kinesthetic sense may be seen in the definition of kinesthetic and tactile perception. As stated previously, kinesthetic perception involves the mental interpretation of the sensation of body movement, whereas tactile perception is concerned with the mental interpretation of what a person experiences through the sense of touch.

Since the tactile and kinesthetic senses are so closely related, the identifying factors of deficiency in kinesthesis previously reported can also be used to determine whether there is a deficiency in the tactile sense.

Many sports activities provide tactile sensitivity. For example, dribbling a basketball gives the feeling of the ball movement and its placement on the floor. This is also valuable as far as *timing* is related to kinesthetic perception. The sport of wrestling, by providing body-to-body contact, has a high level of tactile sensitivity. Also, gymnastic activities that have children come in contact with the surface area or piece of apparatus have this same quality.

At a very high level of sports activity—such as professional football—the television viewer will perhaps have noticed that two or more offensive linemen (not on the home team) will be holding hands. The reason for this is that the players away from the center cannot hear the quarterback's signals because of the crowd noise. At the snap of the ball the inside lineman will release the hand of his teammate. In this situation the tactile sense becomes a medium of communication.

In studying tactile perception, Raviv and Zehavit found that physical activity (such as that found in sports) can provide a supportive treatment framework in touch perception, and make children aware of their bodies' boundaries as they develop a positive physical image.[3]

Visual and Auditory Perception

The visual and auditory systems provide two of the most important forms of input for learning. The term *visual* is concerned with images that are obtained through the eyes. Thus, visual input involves the various learning media directed to the visual sense. The term *auditory* may be described as stimulation occurring through the sense organs of hearing. Therefore, auditory input is concerned with the various learning media directed to the auditory sense.

These two forms of sensory input complement each other in individuals who have both normal vision and hearing. However, as the extremes away from normalcy are approached, as in the case of complete or near-complete absence of one of the senses, their use as combined learning media obviously diminishes. However, at the extremes of normalcy, a person relies a great deal upon the system which is functioning normally. For example, although the sightless person relies a great deal upon tactile perception, particularly as far as "reading" is concerned, he or she is also extremely sensitive to auditory input in the form of various sounds. In a similar manner, the hearing-impaired person relies heavily upon the visual sense as a form of sensory input.

The relationship of these two senses in children with normal or near-normal functioning of both senses is seen in the area of reading. There is a natural sequence from listening to reading, and the acquisition of the skill of auditory discrimination is an important factor in learning to read. In addition, in many sports teaching-learning situations these two forms of sensory input are used in combination. For example, the coach might use oral communication to describe shooting a basketball, demonstrating the skill at the same time. Of course, one of the important features for coaches to consider is the extent to which these aspects of sensory input should be used simultaneously. The coach needs to be aware of how well a certain group of children can handle two tasks together (explanation and demonstration). In other words, if visual and auditory input are combined in a sports teaching-learning situation, the coach must determine whether and to what extent one becomes an attention-distracting factor for the other.

Visual Perception. This form of sensory input is the mental interpretation of what a person sees. A number of aspects of visual perception that have been identified include eye-motor coordination, figure-ground perception, form constancy, position in space, and spatial relationships. It has been suggested that children who show deficiency in these various areas may have difficulty in school performance. Various training programs have been devised to help correct or improve these conditions in children, with the idea that such training would result in the improvement of learning ability. The extent to which this has been accomplished has been extolled by some but seriously questioned by others. Research involving this general type of training does not present clear-cut and definitive evidence to support the notion that such training results in academic achievement.

Any number of sports experiences provide for improvement of visual perception particularly as it is concerned with *visualization* and *visual-motor coordination*. Visualization involves visual image, which is the mental construction of a visual experience, or the result of mentally combining a number of visual experiences. Visual-motor coordination is concerned with visual-motor tasks that involve the integration of vision and movement. Think about those sports where we are continually admonishing, "Keep your eye on the ball," or "Look the ball into your hands."

The following activities can be used for sports practice drills to help children improve on visual perception. Again, these activities can carry over into the more complex sports activities.

In the game Jump the Shot the children form a circle, with one child standing in the center holding a length of rope with an object tied to one end. The object should be something soft such as a beanbag. The player in the center starts the game by swinging the object on the rope around and around, close to the feet of the players forming the circle. The players in the circle attempt to avoid being hit by the object by jumping over it when it goes by them. A point can be scored against any person hit on the feet by the object on the rope. This activity provides a good opportunity for visual-motor coordination, as a child must quickly coordinate his or her movement with the visual experience. This can be a good evaluation technique for the coach since it can be seen how well a child makes the judgment necessary to jump over the object at the proper time.

In the game Ball Pass the players are divided into two or more groups and each group forms a circle. The object of the game is to pass the ball around the circle to see which group can get it around first. The coach gives the direction for the ball to be passed from one player to another. For example, the coach may say, "Pass the ball to the right," "Toss the ball over two players," and so on. The game may be varied by using more than one ball of different sizes and different weights. For instance a basketball, volleyball, and tennis ball might be used. This activity provides a good opportunity to improve eye-hand coordination, and it has been observed that after practice in this activity poor coordination can be improved.

In Keep It Up children are divided into several small circles, with each circle having a volleyball. On a signal, one child tosses the ball into the air and the other children try to see how long they can keep the ball up without letting it touch the floor. The group that keeps it up in the air for the longest time is the winner. This activity can be used for the improvement of eye-hand coordination.

Auditory Perception. My studies show that about 75 percent of our waking hours are spent communicating. Of this time, 45 percent is spent in listening, 20 percent in speaking, 16 percent in reading, and 9 percent in writing. If this can be used as a valid criterion, the importance of developing listening skills cannot be denied. If children are going to learn to listen effectively, care should be taken to improve upon their auditory perception—the mental interpretation of what a person hears.

Sports activities provide numerous opportunities for the improvement of auditory perception. In games such as football, where signals are verbalized, success is dependent upon the auditory clues. Also during participation players receive auditory input from the coach and other players in the form of directions.

The following activities can be used as sports practice drills to sharpen the auditory perception in children.

In the game of Stoop Tag children form a circle and join hands. One child is "It" and stands in the center of the circle. The children walk around the circle saying. "I am happy, I am free! I am down, you can't catch me!" At the word "down," the children stoop and let go of one another's hands. Then they stand and jump and hop about, daring the child who is "It" to tag them. They must stoop to avoid being tagged. If a child is tagged when not stooping, he or she becomes "It."

Children first learn to act on the basis of verbal instructions by others. Later, they learn to guide and direct their own behavior on the basis of their own language—they literally talk to themselves, giving themselves instructions. This point of view has long been supported by research, starting with the early work of Luria, which postulated that speech is a form of communication between children and adults and that later becomes a means of organizing the child's own behavior.[4] This means that the function which was previously divided between two people—child and adult—later becomes a function of human behavior. The point of Stoop Tag is that the child tells himself or herself what to do and then does it. The child says, "I am down," and then carries out this action.

In the game of Dog Chase, children are divided into five or six groups. The members of each group are given the name of a breed of dog, such as collie, poodle, and so on. The small groups then mingle into one large group. One child, acting as the leader, throws a ball or other object away from the group, at the same time calling out one of the dog names. All of the children with this dog name run after the object. The one who gets possession of it first becomes the leader for the next time. The coach can use this activity as a diagnostic technique by observing those children who react slowly or do not react at all to the auditory input.

In closing this final chapter, I come full circle by repeating the theme made at the outset. Development of children through sports does not accrue automatically. However, there is a great potential for this to occur if adults who become involved in children's sports do so in the best interest of the children physically, socially, emotionally, and intellectually.

Notes

Chapter 1

1. Good, Carter V., *Dictionary of Education,* Second Edition, New York, McGraw-Hill Book Company, 1959, p. 167.

Chapter 2

1. Nelson, Gary D., Effects of Preschool Health Education Curriculum on Children's Health Knowledge, Research Abstracts, American Alliance for Healthy Physical Education, Recreation, and Dance, Reston, VA, 1988.

2. Cousins, Norman, *The Healing Heart,* New York, W. W. Norton and Company, 1983, p. 66.

3. Hart, Archibald D., *Stress and Your Child,* Dallas, Wood Publishing Company, 1992, p. 87.

4. "Mini Page," *The Washington Post,* December 25, 1988, p. 10.

5. Kaufman, Marc, Workshop Takes Pulse of Sleep Teens, *Health,* September 21, 1999, p. 7.

Chapter 3

1. Selye, Hans, *Stress Without Distress,* New York, Signet New American Library, p. 18.

2. In discussing the stress concept I do not intend to get into a highly technical discourse on the complex aspect of stress. Nonetheless, certain basic understandings need to be taken into account, and this requires the use of some technical terms. For this reason I am providing a list of terms and definitions that are used in the discussion.

ACTH (adrenocorticotropic hormone): A hormone secreted by the pituitary gland. It influences the function of the adrenals and other glands in the body.

adrenaline: A hormone secreted by the medulla of the adrenal glands.

adrenals: Two glands in the upper posterior part of the abdomen that produce and secrete hormones. They have two parts, the outer layer, called the cortex, and the inner core, called the medulla.

corticoids: Hormones produced by the adrenal cortex, an example of which is cortisone.

endocrine glands: Glands that secrete their hormones into the bloodstream.

hormone: A chemical produced by a gland and secreted into the bloodstream, which then influences the function of cells or organs.

hypothalamus: The primary activator of the autonomic nervous system, it plays a central role in translating neurological stimuli into endocrine processes during stress reactions.

pituitary: A pea-sized endocrine gland located at the base of the brain. It secretes important hormones, including ACTH.

thymus: A ductless gland that is considered a part of the endocrine gland system, located behind the upper part of the breast bone.

3. Johnston, Carol A., *Families in Stress,* Department of Health and Human Services, Washington, DC, HHS Publications, No. (OHDS) 80-301-30162, p. 3.

4. Swain, C. J., Stress As a Factor in Primary School Children's Reading Problems, doctoral dissertation, North Texas State University, Denton, TX, 1985.

5. Brown, Bernard, and Rosenbaum, Lilian, Stress and Competence, *Stress in Childhood,* edited by James H. Humphrey, New York, AMS Press, Inc., 1984, pp. 117-154.

Chapter 4

1. Horney, Karen, *The Neurotic Personality of Our Times,* New York, W. W. Norton and Company, Inc., 1937.

2. Kohn, A., *No Contest: The Case Against Competition,* Boston, Houghton-Mifflin, 1986, p. 16.

3. Scanlan, Tara K., and Passer, M. W., *The Psychological and Social Affects of Competition,* Los Angeles, University of California, 1977.

4. Scanlan, Tara K., Social Psychological Aspects of Competition for Male Youth Sports Participation: Predictors of Competitive Stress, *Journal of Sports Psychology,* 6, 1984, p. 23.

5. Bowen, Fred, Three Sad Tales, *Kidspost,* August 31, 2001, p. 16.

6. Orland, R. G., Soccer-Related Eye Injuries in Children and Adolescents, *Physician and Sportsmedicine,* November 1988, p. 27.

7. Requests for materials may be sent to Little League Baseball, Inc., Box 3485, Williamsport, PA 17701.

8. Sewell, Dan, Are Parents Ruining the Game? West Palm, FL, *Youth Sports Coach,* Fall 1992, p. 14.

9. Dotson, C. O., Criteria Reference Standard: Aerobic Fitness, *Journal of Physical Education, Recreation, and Dance,* September 1988, p. 112.

10. Rikli, Roberta E., Petray, Claire, and Baumgartner, Ted A., The Reliability of Distance Run Tests for Children in Grades K-4, *Research Quarterly for Exercise and Sports,* September 1992, p. 97.

Chapter 5

1. Good, Carter V., *Dictionary of Education,* Second Edition, New York, McGraw-Hill Book Company, 1959, p. 172.

Chapter 6

1. Martens, Rainer, et al., A Field Study of Traditional and Nontraditional Children's Baseball, *Research Quarterly for Exercise and Sports,* December 1984, p. 17.

Chapter 7

1. Good, Carter V., *Dictionary of Education,* Second Edition, New York, McGraw-Hill Book Company, 1959, p. 168.

2. Chase, Melissa A., and Dummer, Gail M., The Role of Sports As a Social Determinant for Children, *Research Quarterly for Exercise and Sports,* December 1992, p. 43.

3. American Sports Education Program, *Sport Parent,* Champaign, IL, Human Kinetics Publisher, Inc., 1994, p. 142.

4. Berlage, G., Are Children's Competitive Team Sports Socializing Agents for Corporate America? Paper presented at the North American Society for Sociology of Sport, Fort Worth, TX, November 12-15, 1981.

5. Donegam, Craig, Sportsmanship Takes a Dive in America, *Youth Sport Coaches,* Winter 1992, p. 4.

Chapter 9

1. Bancroft, Jessie H., *Games,* New York, The MacMillan Company, 1909, p. 9.

2. Whiting, H. T. A., *Personality and Performance in Physical Education and Sport,* London, Henry Kimpton, 1973, p. 135.

3. Raviv, S., and Zehavit, L., The Importance of Touch Perception in Early Childhood and Its Implications in Physical Activity, *Journal of the International Council for Health, Physical Education, Recreation, Sport, and Dance,* Reston, VA, Spring 1997, p. 42.

4. Luria, A. R., Development of the Directive Function of Speech in Early Childhood, *Word,* 1959, p. 15.

Index

SPECIAL 25%-OFF DISCOUNT!
Order a copy of this book with this form or online at:
http://www.haworthpressinc.com/store/product.asp?sku=4834

CHILD DEVELOPMENT THROUGH SPORTS

_____in hardbound at $22.46 (regularly $29.95) (ISBN: 0-7890-1827-6)

_____in softbound at $13.46 (regularly $17.95) (ISBN: 0-7890-1828-4)

Or order online and use Code HEC25 in the shopping cart.

COST OF BOOKS_____

OUTSIDE US/CANADA/
MEXICO: ADD 20%_____

POSTAGE & HANDLING_____
(US: $5.00 for first book & $2.00
for each additional book)
Outside US: $6.00 for first book
& $2.00 for each additional book)

SUBTOTAL_____

IN CANADA: ADD 7% GST_____

STATE TAX_____
(NY, OH & MN residents, please
add appropriate local sales tax)

FINAL TOTAL_____
(If paying in Canadian funds,
convert using the current
exchange rate, UNESCO
coupons welcome)

☐ **BILL ME LATER:** ($5 service charge will be added)
(Bill-me option is good on US/Canada/Mexico orders only;
not good to jobbers, wholesalers, or subscription agencies.)

☐ Check here if billing address is different from
shipping address and attach purchase order and
billing address information.

Signature_____

☐ **PAYMENT ENCLOSED: $**_____

☐ **PLEASE CHARGE TO MY CREDIT CARD.**

☐ Visa ☐ MasterCard ☐ AmEx ☐ Discover
☐ Diner's Club ☐ Eurocard ☐ JCB

Account # _____

Exp. Date_____

Signature_____

Prices in US dollars and subject to change without notice.

NAME_____

INSTITUTION_____

ADDRESS_____

CITY_____

STATE/ZIP_____

COUNTRY_____ COUNTY (NY residents only)_____

TEL_____ FAX_____

E-MAIL_____

May we use your e-mail address for confirmations and other types of information? ☐ Yes ☐ No
We appreciate receiving your e-mail address and fax number. Haworth would like to e-mail or fax special
discount offers to you, as a preferred customer. **We will never share, rent, or exchange your e-mail address
or fax number.** We regard such actions as an invasion of your privacy.

Order From Your Local Bookstore or Directly From
The Haworth Press, Inc.
10 Alice Street, Binghamton, New York 13904-1580 • USA
TELEPHONE: 1-800-HAWORTH (1-800-429-6784) / Outside US/Canada: (607) 722-5857
FAX: 1-800-895-0582 / Outside US/Canada: (607) 722-6362
E-mailto: getinfo@haworthpressinc.com
PLEASE PHOTOCOPY THIS FORM FOR YOUR PERSONAL USE.
http://www.HaworthPress.com   BOF02